How to Start Your Own Cybersecurity Consulting Business

The burnout rate of a Chief Information Security Officer (CISO) is pegged at about 16 months. In other words, that is what the average tenure of a CISO is at a business. At the end of their stay, many CISOs look for totally different avenues of work, or they try something else – namely starting their own Cybersecurity Consulting business. Although a CISO might have the skill and knowledge set to go it alone, it takes careful planning to launch a successful Cyber Consulting business. This ranges all the way from developing a business plan to choosing the specific area in Cybersecurity that they want to serve.

How to Start Your Own Cybersecurity Consulting Business: First-Hand Lessons from a Burned-Out Ex-CISO is written by an author who has real-world experience in launching a Cyber Consulting company. It is all-encompassing, with coverage spanning from selecting which legal formation is most suitable to which segment of the Cybersecurity industry should be targeted. The book is geared specifically towards the CISO that is on the verge of a total burnout or career change. It explains how CISOs can market their experience and services to win and retain key customers. It includes a chapter on how certification can give a Cybersecurity consultant a competitive edge and covers the five top certifications in information security: CISSP, CompTIA Security+, CompTIA CySA+, CSSP, and CISM.

The book's author has been in the IT world for more than 20 years and has worked for numerous companies in corporate America. He has experienced CISO burnout. He has also started two successful Cybersecurity companies. This book offers his own unique perspective based on his hard-earned lessons learned and shows how to apply them in creating a successful venture. It also covers the pitfalls of starting a consultancy, how to avoid them, and how to bounce back from any that prove unavoidable. This is the book for burned-out former CISOs to rejuvenate themselves and their careers by launching their own consultancies.

How to Start Your Own Cybersecurity Consulting Business

First-Hand Lessons from a Burned-Out Ex-CISO

Ravi Das

CRC Press
Taylor & Francis Group
Boca Raton London New York

CRC Press is an imprint of the
Taylor & Francis Group, an **informa** business

AN AUERBACH BOOK

First Edition published 2023
by CRC Press
6000 Broken Sound Parkway NW, Suite 300, Boca Raton, FL 33487-2742

and by CRC Press
4 Park Square, Milton Park, Abingdon, Oxon, OX14 4RN
CRC Press is an imprint of Taylor & Francis Group, LLC

ISBN: 978-1-032-30483-0 (hbk)
ISBN: 978-1-032-16363-5 (pbk)
ISBN: 978-1-003-30530-9 (ebk)

DOI: 10.1201/9781003305309

Typeset in Garamond
by Deanta Global Publishing Services, Chennai, India

This book is dedicated to my Lord and Savior, Jesus Christ. It is also dedicated in loving memory to Dr. Gopal Das and Mrs. Kunda Das.

This book is also dedicated to the following individuals and their respective families:

Tim Auckley
Patricia Auckley
Rory Maxfield
Gary Minta
Jaya Chandra
Andre Kostylev

Contents

Acknowledgments

I would like to thank John Wyzalek, my editor, for his help and guidance in the preparation of this book.

About the Author

Ravi Das is a Cybersecurity Consultant and Business Development Specialist and does Cybersecurity Consulting through his private practice, RaviDas.Tech, Inc. He is also studying for his CompTIA Security+ Certification.

Chapter 1

Introduction – The CISO

About Myself

Well, here we go, I am working on my ninth book now, which is this one. I have been writing and publishing books through CRC Press for the past seven years. My first three were on Biometrics, and the remainder were on Cybersecurity. The latter included titles on Web App Security, AI, Cybersecurity Risk and Cyber Insurance, Cloud Security, the Cybersecurity Lessons learned from the COVID-19 pandemic. All of these books were very technical in detail, with a very niche audience.

So, when I approached my editor for thoughts on a new book, he suggested that I come up with something that might be more relevant to the business world. After thinking up ideas, we finally agreed on me to write a book on how to launch a Cybersecurity Consulting business. Even to this day, I have no idea how we came up with this title, but here it is. This is the book.

Apart from being a Technical Writer for the past 13 years, I have been an entrepreneur as well. I started my first business back in the early 2000s, which involved selling Biometric devices. This included both a Hand Geometry Scanner and a

DOI: 10.1201/9781003305309-1

Fingerprint Recognition reader. As I started, I had help along the way, but for the most part, I was on my own. I had to somehow make a living selling these devices.

At first, I thought these would be an easy sell, because I launched this business right after the horrific incidents of 9/11. But I quickly realized that people were much more infatuated with the technology, because it seemed to be so "sexy", rather than deploying it to secure their businesses. As a result, I found that I was spending much more time educating people about what Biometrics is all about, rather than actually selling the products themselves.

Although I didn't see anything wrong with this even though I wasn't making any money off it, it was an educational process to me. For example, I learned a lot more about the human personality, what makes them tick, and most importantly, what their pain points were when it came to security. Of course, I further refined my own skills as well, as I was learning a lot more about Biometrics, in general, and even understanding how to teach people about concepts that were once foreign to me.

This all culminated when I gave a presentation about Biometrics to the Electronic Crimes Task Force of the United States Secret Service of the Chicago Field Office. It was very well received, and in fact, I even got a letter of commendation straight from the Special Agent in Charge. So, while it was great to give presentations and teach people about Biometrics, I still hadn't sold very much; so, I realized as a business owner, I need to change my sales strategies fast.

Although I do have an MBA and I took courses in Marketing, no course could teach you this. I had to change tactics, and fast. In other words, I had to learn through the school of hard knocks on this one. Luckily, during my time of networking and giving presentations, I had made a good network of friends and advisors, and they gave me some advice on what to do next in terms of a sales tactic: Write good content.

I asked them, what does it mean? Well, it simply meant writing content that I was passionate about, and somehow, somewhere, getting it published. Of course, Biometrics was my passion, so there was no issue about finding that out. But the next issue came up: Where would I publish? At the time, I was a member of the Chicago Software Association and the Technology Executives Club, two leading IT groups that were dominant in the Chicago area. I had asked them if they could publish some of these articles, and quite enthusiastically (and even to my surprise), they agreed to. So, the first few articles were about the various Biometric technologies, and in a layman's term, what they were all about. Two of the articles, believe it or not, got some acclamation from around the world. These were about Retinal Recognition and Iris Recognition.

The latter actually got the most attention, as I included a case study about the famous National Geographic picture of the Afghan girl Sharbat Gula and her piercing green eyes that caught the attention of the world during the height of the Afghanistan crisis. Michael McCurry, the photographer who captured these images, was able to locate her again, all through the use of Iris Recognition.

Because of the traction these articles were getting, I kept continuing to write more. I kept more recognition, and alas, I was now writing articles and even, yes, getting paid for it. I remember two of these clients were a security vendor out in the state of New York and the other was located way overseas, in the Netherlands. Although it was great finally getting paid, the revenue and the cash flow that was coming in were still too low to make a true living off.

So, after about 9 years, I had to let go of this company, called HTG Solutions. While it was a sad moment for me, I learned a lot about how to run a business, all by myself, and as mentioned, no MBA class could ever teach you. I was responsible for everything, ranging from the prospecting to the marketing, the accounting, creating contracts, meeting with potential clients, networking, computing taxes (luckily I had a business accountant), you name it.

But most importantly, I learned what I was most passionate about – writing about security. So, I decided that, after closing down HTG Solutions, I would look for a corporate job in this arena. I did land on one, and it was being a Creative Executive for essentially a spam email company (although truly a legitimate one) called eMedia Communications, LLC.

In this role, I would write the copy for all of the content assets that a client would give to the sales representative, and from there, which was handed down to me. I would write the Call To Action (CTA) as well, with a link to the downloadable asset. These copies were then placed onto the relevant bulletins and blasted out on a weekly basis. The company had about 80 such bulletins, and some 3 million-plus opt-in subscribers (which made the spamming legal).

My stuff was placed in all of the IT bulletins. So, whichever subscriber would download, this asset would become a potential sales lead, and this was transmitted off to the client on a prescribed timetable so they could follow up with these sales prospects and hopefully negotiate a deal. So along with being a copywriting job, this also became a lead generation job. But the real-world duties of this job were far more intense and complex than the example just painted.

Over time, I became responsible for handling all of the big-name clients, which included the likes of Autonomy (a division of Hewlett Packard), Seagate (formerly I365), Box, Nimsoft, etc. In other words, I had all of the big-name clients under my belt. My writing skills were now getting honed in, especially from a copywriting perspective.

So, during this timeframe, I thought to myself, I finally found my niche, so maybe why not try to launch HTG Solutions once again, but this time, two things would be different: No products would be sold, and it would be a pure writing business. Well, after consulting with several business attorneys, I finally picked one that I felt comfortable working with, and in March 2009, the new company was born. I won't get into all of the details of this one, but it's been around now for 13 years, and with it, my technical writing has shifted from writing about Biometrics to all things Cyber and related.

Heck, I even have gone into other areas of Cyber as well, which includes consulting. The name of all of these now falls under my private practice name of RaviDas.Tech. You may be asking how is this all relevant? Well, it is from the standpoint that I am still responsible for almost everything, even though I have a new business partner. The experiences that I have gained from HTG Solutions have now been multiplied by a factor of 100 through RaviDas.Tech. I have learned more about running and sustaining a business more, once again, than any MBA program could ever teach.

What I have been through has been real-world and through the school of ultra-hard knocks. My revenue is directly dependent upon how well I write and keep my clients happy. In other words, I am purely and 100% responsible for my own paycheck, which, while rewarding, can be scary at times as well. So, this is how the idea for this book came into being, as I stated before.

My editor essentially told me that since I have so much real-world experience in starting a business, why not create and launch a book that describes how to actually go in detail into starting a Cyber Consulting business? I scratched my head on this one, and after doing some searches on Google and Amazon, there were already plenty of books written on this subject matter. After further consultation with my editor, we decided that the differentiating angle on this one would be written from the perspective of a Chief Information Security Officer (CISO) who is totally burned from their corporate job or just got fired.

Why this specific title, you may be asking? Well, the Cybersecurity Threat Landscape has gotten to the point where it is so complicated, and newer threat variants are coming out on an almost minute-by-minute basis. If something happens, who is the first person to get blamed? Yep, you got it, the CISO. In today's Cyber world, unfortunately, there is still no level of accountability that is established – all fingers first point to the CISO, and then questions get asked later.

So as a result of all this, this poor soul is always in search of greener pastures. So far, the best one to take is to have your own Cyber Consulting business. Now keep in mind, I have never been truly a CISO. If I ever had any major problems, I always went to the Geeks Squad. But as I have said on numerous occasions, I do have that real-world experience. So, for the purposes of this book, I will take that knowledge and assume the role of either burned out or fired CISO in such of those proverbial greener pasture and describe to you all of the details as to what it takes to launch a successful Cyber Consulting business.

But first, it is important to unearth the stresses that a CISO undergoes on a daily basis and why this particular role is so much at risk today. But before we delve into all of that, it is first important to understand what the C-Suite is truly all about.

What the C-Suite Is

For most of us who have been in Corporate America, and even elsewhere around the world, the term "C-Suite" is very familiar. But for those who may not know what it really is, these are the C-level executives who run the company, in a supposedly top-down manner (but that hardly ever exists anymore). Essentially, these are the leaders who the employees ultimately look up to for direction as to how the company should be run.

In the end, the buck stops with the C-Suite. They are supposedly the ones who make the final decisions and approve any budgets that are requested. While this is, of course, a huge responsibility, the image of them is actually kind of negative. The C-Suite is often viewed to be aloof and not caring about anything except to make sure that the Earnings Per Share (EPS) has increased and that they are filling up their fat coffers with bonuses and more stock options.

While this may be true in the Fortune 500, this is far from it for the Small- to Medium-Sized businesses (also known as "SMBs"). In fact, I know many C-Suite members in this regard, and many of them are very caring individuals not only for the welfare of their businesses but also for their employees. So, this image as just described really depends upon a lot on the size, kind, and type of industry the business in question is.

But here is one fact that is well known, at least here in the Cybersecurity Industry. Many members of the C-Suite simply do not understand what Cyber threats or risks really are, and more often than not, they really don't care. In fact, even the CISO has a very hard time trying to get a line of communications up and running with the other members of the C-Suite, and this is even one of the prime reasons why the burnout rate for them is so high.

But, this is a topic that will be examined later in this chapter. But before we move on any further, it is first important to define what the roles of each member of the C-Suite are, and how in theory, at least, their contribution is made to the company that they are leading.

The C-Suite Roles

Here they are, as follows:

1) *The Chief Executive Officer (CEO)*

This role is deemed to be the most significant, as this person is viewed as the captain of the ship and is responsible for setting the vision, goals, plans, and budgets for the company. The CEO is pretty much responsible for everything, and if something goes wrong, of course, they will be the first ones to get blamed, and fired. In fact, all of the other members of the C-Suite report to this particular individual. But more specifically, here are their typical roles:

■ Communicating, on behalf of the company, with shareholders, government entities, and the public
■ Leading the development of the company's short- and long-term strategy
■ Creating and implementing the company or organization's vision and mission
■ Evaluating the work of other executive leaders within the company, including directors, vice presidents, and presidents
■ Maintaining awareness of the competitive market landscape, expansion opportunities, industry developments, etc.
■ Ensuring that the company maintains high social responsibility wherever it does business
■ Assessing risks to the company and ensuring they are monitored and minimized
■ Setting strategic goals and making sure they are measurable and describable

(Source: 1)

2) *The Chief Financial Officer*
As the title implies, this particular individual is primarily responsible for all of the financial activities that happen from within the business. This includes setting up and approving budgets, figuring out where every dollar and cent has gone to, doing audits among the various departments, and even working with regulators and auditors in case of any issue with money laundering, internal fraud, etc. Heck, this individual even has to answer directly to the IRS if there are any questions about the

corporate tax returns that have been filed. Also, if the company wants to buy out another company in Merger and Acquisition (M and A) activity, they have to give the final approval, at least from the money allocation standpoint. More specifically, here are their job functions:

- Reporting

    Reporting takes up a lot of a CFO's time, and this responsibility typically resides in the Controller's group. This team of professionals prepares all of the company's historical financial reports required for shareholders, employees, lenders, research analysts, governments, and regulatory bodies. This group is responsible for ensuring all reporting is prepared in an accurate and timely manner.

- Liquidity

    The CFO needs to ensure the company is able to meet its financial commitments and manage cash flow in the most efficient way. These responsibilities are usually carried out by the treasury group, which is often smaller than the reporting team. This group is tasked with managing the company's cash balance and working capital, such as accounts payable, accounts receivable, and inventory. They also carry out the issuing of any debt, managing investments, and handle other liquidity-related decisions.

- Return on Investment

    The third thing a CFO does is help the company earn the highest possible risk-adjusted return on assets and return on capital (or return on equity). This is where the financial planning and analysis – FP&A team – comes in to help the CFO forecast future cash flow of the business and then compare actual results to what was budgeted. The

FP&A team plays a critical role in analytics and decision making in the business.

If the company has a corporate development team, they also play a big part in creating (or attempting to create) optimal investment returns for the business.

(Source: 2)

3) *The Chief Operating Officer (COO)*

This particular individual is tasked with making sure that all of the visions and plans that have been set forth by the CEO are actually implemented to whatever degree that is possible and also making sure that the money is there to fund each project as allocated by the CFO. This position is very often viewed as being the "second in command", meaning, if anything happens to the CEO, the COO will then assume that role to ensure that there is a seamless transfer of power. Also, the COO is ultimately responsible for the functioning of each department within the company. More specifically, their job roles are as follows:

> The chief operating officer's job revolves entirely around the CEO's wants and needs. Whatever operational tasks need to be accomplished, the COO makes sure that they are done. It usually involves working with the heads or teams of overseers working in each department (e.g., IT, finance, marketing). A COO is responsible for making sure that all the departments work together to keep the operations of the business on schedule.
>
> The chief operating officer often holds regular meetings with the heads of each department to make sure that operations are running smoothly and that any issue

is addressed immediately. In addition, the COO is often the intermediary between the heads of departments, making sure that they communicate with one another when a project requires more than one department to work together.

(Source: 3)

Thus, it is very important to keep in mind that the above three roles are common to all businesses. This simply means that these are the most vital C-Suite roles in a company, and won't be taken away. But interestingly enough, once again depending upon the scope and size of the business and the industry that they serve, more roles can be added to the above list, which include the following:

- Chief Brand Officer
- Chief Commercial Officer
- Chief Data Officer
- Chief Human Resources Officer
- Chief Investment Officer
- Chief Legal Officer
- Chief Medical Officer
- Chief Research Officer
- Chief Security Officer
- Chief Strategy Officer

The Role of the Chief Information Officer (CIO)

Now, the role of what this book is about does not appear in this list, at least not yet. It will be discussed later in this chapter. But, it is often viewed that the role of the CISO often stems from that of the Chief Information Office (CIO). This role is very often referred to as that of the Chief Technology

Officer, or simply "CTO" for short. The role of this position is to oversee the technological developments that are happening in their company, past, present, and future. Their job is purely from a business perspective, not the nerdy kind of work that you would expect to see from a Project Manager of a software development team.

The breakdown of the role of the CIO can be seen below:

From a short-term perspective

- Approving the purchase of information technology equipment: CIOs are responsible for monitoring the IT department's budget and deciding whether and how to procure the necessary equipment.
- Delegating tasks to increase productivity: As a part of their job responsibilities, a CIO is responsible for taking a large project and dividing it into segments for separate departments to work on.
- Managing the IT department and employees: CIOs are expected to manage all employees who work within the IT department. They answer employee questions, monitor overall department progress and ensure that every employee is exhibiting a productive work ethic.
- Overseeing new network and system implementations: They're responsible for planning and overseeing each step in the implementation process with the help of the IT director and tech department managers. Common projects include deploying new CMS systems and ensuring security compliance.

From a long-term perspective

- Developing business relationships with IT vendors: A CIO maintains a healthy relationship with vendors and suppliers who produce or manufacture

IT devices for corporate use. This can be useful in learning about new technologies before their competitors.

■ Staying abreast of industry trends and new IT technologies: CIOs keep up with changes in information technology. They often read reports and studies on new technologies that could be of use to the company's internal processes or communication channels, ensuring the organization remains competitive.

■ Strategizing and creating solutions specific to the company's needs: CIOs might be asked to create tailor-made technology solutions that cater directly to the company and employee productivity. This might include creating a special CMS system or coming up with remote working solutions."

■ Working closely with other company executives to determine best practices: They're responsible for collaborating with their executive counterparts to discuss issues, improvements or information to be disseminated to employees.

(Source: 6)

Just before the COVID-19 pandemic hit a couple of years ago, there were often a lot of questions asked if the role of CISO is directly reportable to that of the CIO, or if the two should be separate. As previously mentioned, the role of the CISO will be further reviewed later in this chapter. But long story short, the primary role of the CISO is to safeguard both the physical and digital assets of the company that they work for.

This question has been going on for some time, and ultimately, it was agreed upon by Corporate America that the role of the CISO would be directly reportable to that of the CIO. But also as mentioned, the Cybersecurity Threat Landscape has grown to levels never expected before. Thus, the role of the CIO has now become pretty much eradicated now in Corporate America. But, in response to this, there is a new role of the CISO that has recently come about, and this is known as the "Virtual CISO", or vCISO for short.

The bottom line here is that instead of having to go through the bother, administrative nightmare, and huge expense of hiring a direct CISO onto your staff, you can hire one for a fixed period of time, for a fixed fee. Thus, this has made the role a very attractive one for businesses in Corporate America. The next section describes this role in more detail.

The Role of the vCISO

The Key Differences between the vCISO and the CISO

First, what exactly is a vCISO? It can be defined as follows:

> He or she is an outsourced security expert who can remotely set up and lead strategic security initiatives for an organization. vCISOs often work for multiple organizations at once to provide strategic security leadership.
>
> **(Source: 7)**

So, as you can see, a vCISO is actually like an independent contractor to whom you have outsourced your CISO functions. This can be an individual who has their own business, or it can be a group of different people in the same organization. They can be hired on a project-by-project basis, or even for the long term, depending upon what your needs are at the present time.

Some of the key differences between the vCISO and hiring an in-house CISO are as follows:

■ The vCISO is much more affordable. You will not have to pay an exorbitant salary and benefits, such as medical insurance and vacation time.
■ The vCISO will not leave you unless you fire them for whatever reason. They will stay with you for the duration for as long as you need them.
■ Because the vCISO is an outsourced, third-party entity, he or she can offer you expert, and unbiased views of what they think you need to get done in terms of launching your Cybersecurity initiatives. For example, this could be the procurement and deployment of brand-new Artificial Intelligence tools all the way on how to craft your Security Policies and Disaster Recovery/Incident Response Plans.
■ Typically, most organizations hire only one in-house CISO. Because of this, he or she is shouldered in assuming all of the Cybersecurity responsibilities, which, in turn, leads to a huge turnover rate. But by using a vCISO, your outsourced entity will already be networked to other resources that can be called upon, if necessary, in order to address all of your Cybersecurity needs.

The Benefits of the vCISO

1) *You get a wide breadth of expertise*
   While your CIO is probably a well-educated individual with deep experience, it does not necessarily mean that they have all the expertise that you need to keep up with the dynamics of the Cyber Threat Landscape. For example, as businesses are letting their workers back in once again, one of the main issues to be dealt with is that of creating and maintaining a rock-solid Business Continuity (BC) Plan. Because of the pandemic, many CIOs and CISOs are now fully understanding the importance of

having this, so that they will be 100% prepared for the next major event. Unfortunately, they may not necessarily have the knowledge in crafting out such a plan. Therefore, you need to reach out to a vCISO who has these specific skills that can help you to create this. You do not have to hire this person on a full-time basis; you can hire them for a fixed time period at a very affordable price. Very likely, this individual will more than likely have other contacts as well that can offer even their own level of expertise to other aspects of your BC Plan.

2) *It is a very cost-effective approach to take*

As it was just described, cash flow is of prime importance to any business, no matter how large or small. Everybody is now on a very tight budget, at unprecedented levels never seen before, and paying your existing CIO is probably out of the question. The average salary for a CIO is now pegged at about almost $270,000.00. Keep in mind that this does not even include benefits, bonuses, stock options, and other perks. When you add all of this together, the entire compensation package can come close to almost $2,000,000.00. In today's times, which business can really afford this? Not many. So, this is where the role of hiring a well-established vCISO will become crucial. In monetary terms, you can save at least 40% by hiring such a person. Best of all, you don't have to pay all of the extras like you would have to for a CIO, all you have to do is pay them for the time that you need them, on a flat fee basis. When your project is done, you can terminate the contract and bring them back on board again on an as-needed basis. As a result, you will have that much more money in your IT budget to spend on other items that you need to shore up your Cybersecurity posture.

3) *You will get an unbiased view*

The C-Suite across Corporate America has often been viewed as a place where company politics often play out.

Because of this, many of the decisions that are made may not necessarily reflect what is best for the business. What you need (and especially right now) is an individual who is not bound by such nuances and who can offer you in precise terms what you need to do right now in order to clean up and improve your current levels of the proverbial cyber hygiene. This is where the role of the vCISO will come into crucial play. In other words, he or she can come right in, conduct an exhaustive assessment of how things are being done right now in your company, and offer you real-world solutions to make things better. Because they are an external resource you have hired, they can provide you with an insight that is completely neutral and what is best for your business.

4) *You can get staff augmentation*

For quite some time now, there has been a severe shortage of skilled workers in the Cybersecurity Industry. Obviously, hiring new, full-time staff could very well be out of the question right now, as you are trying to keep up with paying your existing staff. But because everybody is so overworked right now, other pressing Cybersecurity needs could literally take a back seat right now. But this does not necessarily have to be the case for your business. For example, if you hire the right kind of vCISO, they can actually augment your current, full-time staff and help them keep up with their daily job tasks. As also mentioned earlier, they will probably have other contacts on board that you can hire as well for a fixed-term contract.

5) *Proactiveness will be a main area of focus*

Although every CIO/CISO, at the bottom of their hearts, would like to have a proactive Cyber mindset that transcends to each and every employee in their business, this is an almost impossible task to do. A primary reason for this is that the burnout rate is so high among them that it is almost impossible to keep them on for the long haul. For example, 91% of CIOs and CISOs across

Corporate America at the present time feel a huge amount of stress, causing them to quit at unprecedented levels. But by hiring an external vCISO, he or she will not feel this to such a high degree, and as a result, they will be able to quickly foster that proactive Cyber mindset and even foster higher levels of motivation among your IT security team that is so badly needed today.

Other Related CISO Roles

As it was mentioned earlier in this chapter, more Cyber-related C-Roles can be added to the C-Suite if and when necessary, given just how dynamic the Cyber Threat Landscape has become. Just like the vCISO, these two roles are of the virtual kind. They are as follows:

■ The Virtual Privacy Officer (vPO)
■ The Virtual Chief Compliance Officer (vCCO)

These two roles deal primarily with the privacy and safety of the Personal Identifiable Information (PII) datasets of both the customers and employees. One of the primary reasons for the emergence of two roles is the birth and enforcement of the two major data privacy laws, which are the GDPR and the CCPA. These two roles are now examined in greater detail in the next two sections.

The Role of the vPO

As its title implies, the vPO is tasked to protect the Personal Identifiable Information (PII) datasets of any business that needs it. But it is simply not just names, addresses, social security numbers, and credit card numbers, and data can have a plethora of different meanings and applications as well.

For example, in the health-care industry, this will very often be the patient medical records that are stored and reside within the various databases of the health-care providers. Or to an online merchant, it could be the various buying patterns of existing customers and the chatbot conversations that are engaged with prospects.

When it comes to the Remote Workforce, there is a lot of confidential data that is transmitted between the remote worker and the servers at the primary location of the business. This could include intelligence information, financial numbers, or ultrasensitive corporate documents. Whatever it may be, it is the primary responsibility of the vPO to ensure they safeguard not only when the data is in transit but also when it is either archived or stored for subsequent usage.

Here are some of the key benefits of hiring a vPO:

1) *Your data will be mapped very quickly and efficiently*

With the vPO, they will be able to walk in within hours in order to inspect your datasets and help you map the inter-linkages that exist within them. As a business owner, if you have not done this before, this can be a very laborious and time-consuming process. Obviously, you will not be able to dedicate an in-house team to do this, as they will be heavily burdened working on their other Cyber-related projects. The vPO that you hire should have a wide breadth of experience in this area, and because of that, they can even provide strategies and recommendations as to how these interlinkages can be made more secure by deploying the right controls. Remember, the Cyberattacker is not just after the data per se, they are also interested in finding any hidden backdoors to which they can penetrate through and exploit your databases even further.

2) *Data intelligence*

To you, all of your datasets are of course very important. But which ones are truly *the most mission-critical* to your business? This is where the vPO can also provide answers. He or she will scan all of the PII and determine which ones are most valuable and needed for your business. For example, they will ask tough questions such as:

    a. How is your business using this PII?

    b. Why is it being stored the way it is?

    c. Where does the data go once it is being accessed?

3) *The categorization of the data*

    Apart from determining what is most valuable to your business, the vPO will also conduct a very thorough and comprehensive risk assessment to see which of your data sets are most at risk for being exposed via a security breach. By doing this, strategies and recommendations will be provided for you as to the kinds of safeguards you can implement to minimize the risk of both non-intentional and intentional exposure.

The Role of the vCCO

Once you have all of your datasets safe and secure, it is now the role of vCCO to make sure that all of the PII that is collected, used, and stored now come into compliance with the extremely rigorous standards that have been set forth by the GDPR and the CCPA.

These pieces of legislation have been set forth to audit businesses, and if they don't come up to snuff, heavy financial penalties can be imposed. Thus, it is one of the primary roles of the vCCO to make sure you are indeed compliant and can avoid the chances of actually being audited.

Some of the key benefits of getting a vCCO are as follows:

1) *Provide overall guidance and support*

    If you do not currently have a data-compliance program, the vCCO can put this into motion for you. Once you know where everything is stored and the interlinkages between them, the next step is then to make sure that whatever you have in place is going to become compliant with the GDPR and the CCPA. For example, the vCCO should possess a deep and intricate knowledge of them, and therefore, they can help you to create a plan to help make sure that whatever clause, statute, or provision affects you, your business is in full, 100% compliance with them. Also, as these laws keep changing, the vCCO will keep your plans updated correspondingly.

2) *Dealing with the governmental agencies*

Let's face it, nobody likes dealing with government regulators because of the amount of paperwork and bureaucracy that is usually involved. Well, it is the job of the vCCO to do these kinds of things for you. They can deal with all of this at the federal, state, and local levels. More than likely, the vCCO and the team that they bring along with them will also probably have contacts with these government agencies as well, which will make the coordination process among all of them for your business a seamless one.

3) *The reporting of issues*

If your business is ever impacted by a Cyberattack, one of the main items of priority that you need to do is to inform all of the governmental agencies that could be involved. This is especially critical as you inform key stakeholders as to what happened and what is being done to rectify the situation. This is one of the first questions that you will be asked by a government auditor if you have done it or not. By having a vCCO on staff, they will make sure that you will follow all of the right channels in this regard, as it can be a very daunting task to accomplish.

4) *Conveying the importance of compliance*

Yes, we all keep hearing about the importance of security training, especially with the advent of the Remote Workforce. But one thing that often gets forgotten about is also training your staff and employees as to what compliance means and the importance of it when it comes to maintaining an acceptable level of Cyber Hygiene.

This kind of training can be very tricky to give, but your vCCO should be able to create a training program that will ultimately convey the importance of this.

The Role of the CISO

As mentioned earlier in the last section of this chapter, the role of the CIO has been overseeing the strategic direction of the company from a technological purpose. But with the world now going pretty much digital all over, their role for the most part is seeing its last days, as the CISO is now taking this role over as well. But apart from that, the CISO is also primarily responsible for overseeing the security and safeguarding of all of the physical and digital assets of their company.

This includes not only making sure that the right security technology tools and technologies are procured but that they are deployed properly and functioning at the most optimal level possible per the security requirements that have been set forth. Not only this, but the CISO is also responsible for making sure that the right controls are put into place and all forms of data leakages are prevented, whether they are intentional or not.

Also, the CISO is charged with whatever has been implemented that comes into compliance with the data privacy laws of such things like the GDPR, the CCPA, HIPAA, etc. If not, they will face the frontline firing squad when it comes to going through an audit and facing any steep financial penalties. So you can get a glimpse now of some of the reasons for the CISO burning out in their respective roles so quickly. But apart from these roles just described, the CISO is also primarily responsible for the following as well, which also lead to the high rate of CISO burnout:

- Security Operations
- Cyber Risk and Cyber Resiliency

- Data Loss
- Internal Fraud Prevention
- Identity and Access Management
- Third-Party and Vendor Risk Management
- Investigations and Forensics
- Governance

These are all examined in the next subsections of this chapter.

Security Operations

This means that the CISO must make sure that all processes are running smoothly and optimally, in both the external and internal environments that their company is facing, from the standpoint of their IT and network infrastructures. This problem has become even further compounded with the evolution of the Remote Workforce, and the permanent foothold it has now taken on Corporate America, driven by the COVID-19 pandemic. Some examples of threats that had to be dealt with included Zoombombing, and the meshing of the corporate and home networks, when employees first started to work from (WFH).

Cyber Risk and Cyber Resiliency

The term "risk" can mean anything to any business. But essentially put, it is how much a business can tolerate from a security breach before they experience a significant and permanent loss in both mission-critical processes and revenues. This next subsection goes into Cyber Risk in more detail, of which the CISO must be aware.

Defining Cyber Risk

Actually, Cybersecurity Risk is composed of three components, which are as follows:

1) *The Threat*

These are the actual Cyber-related threats that your business faces on a daily basis. For example, this can include Ransomware, Phishing, Social Engineering, Malware, Trojan Horses, you name it. For each level of threat that you have or are hypothetically expected to go through, you need to assign a numerical score, using a range, perhaps of 1–10. So, if you have experienced numerous Phishing attacks, you would probably rank that threat vector as a 9 or a 10.

2) *The Vulnerability*

It is very important for your organization to conduct what is known as a "Risk Analysis". With this, you are taking a very close look as to what all of your assets are, both digital- and physical-based. Once you accomplish this, then you need to rate each one on a categorization scale, using 1–10 as an example. Obviously, those assets which you and your IT security team deem to be the most vulnerable will have a higher ranking, and those that are the least vulnerable will have a lower ranking. So, for instance, if your analysis shows that your servers are still potentially highly vulnerable, you would assign again as either a 9 or a 10.

3) *The Consequence*

In this variable, you actually try to quantify the financial loss that your business will experience in the wake of a security breach. Of course, you will want this downtime to be as minimal as possible, and you will want to resume mission-critical processes in just a very short period of time. But no matter what the timeframe is, it is absolutely crucial that you ascertain the amount of revenue that will disappear. In this scenario, you really cannot utilize the categorization scale of 1–10, because you will be assigning a specific dollar value to it, which can vary. For example, if you think your downtime will be about 4 hours to your primary

server from a Phishing attack, then you would potentially assign a dollar amount of $10,000.00 of financial
losses. But it is also very important to keep in mind
that this variable also consists of other losses that are
much more subjective to quantify. These will primarily
include those costs that will result from after the fact
which can be:

a. Brand loss
b. Reputational loss
c. Loss of customers
d. Gaining new customers
e. Expenses associated with potential lawsuits
f. Potential fines for noncompliance (which will come
   from either the GDPR or the CCPA)
g. Costs of free credit reports to those customers that
   have been impacted, etc.

In the end, taking all of the above factors into consideration,
Cybersecurity Risk all comes down to how much damage you
can withstand for a short period of time. Companies that are
much larger in terms of both revenue and employees will have
a much larger risk, whereas those entities that are smaller in
nature will obviously have a much lower threshold to it.

How to Manage Cybersecurity Risk

Now that you have an understanding of what it is, the next
step is implementing those steps to properly manage your
company's tolerance to it. Here are some key items to consider in this regard:

1) *Develop a Cybersecurity culture*
   By this, you are making your company adopt an overall, proactive mindset about the threat variants that are
   out there. It starts all the way from the top from the
   C-Suite to all the way down to your after-hours cleaning

crew. The common line of thinking here is that it is the IT department that should be responsible for all of this, but this is completely false. Each and every employee has their own set of responsibilities to make sure all assets remain safe.

2) *You have to share what you know*

This simply means that you make all of your departments aware of what the Cyber Threat Landscape is looking out there and that you share the information that you have with others. Of course, not every employee needs to know all of the details, only the relevant ones, which will include the managers and higher-up titles. Taking this kind of approach will help to stimulate the proactive mindset as just previously alluded to.

3) *Maintaining strong levels of Cyber Hygiene*

This refers to the fact as to how well all of your employees can recognize a Cyberattack and play their part in helping to contain it. This can involve the following:

a. Learning how to spot a Phishing email;
b. How not to fall for a Social Engineering Attack;
c. Logging into the corporate network in a secure manner (if your employee is working remotely);
d. Creating and maintaining difficult-to-break passwords (such as making use of a password manager);
e. Reporting any anomalous or unusual behavior to the IT security team (in this instance, you will want to maintain a $24 \times 7 \times 365$ direct hotline).

Another key area which the CISO must deal with is known as Cyber Resiliency. This term has often been confused with Cyber Risk, but it merely refers to how well their organization can bounce back after they have been hit by a Security Breach. The next subsection of this chapter examines this in more detail.

Introduction – What Exactly Is Cyber Resiliency?

A technical definition of it is as follows:

> Cyber resilience is the ability to prepare for, respond to and recover from cyberattacks. It helps an organization protect against cyber risks, defend against, and limit the severity of attacks, and ensure its continued survival despite an attack. Cyber resilience has emerged over the past few years because traditional cyber security measures are no longer enough to protect organizations from the spate of persistent attacks.

(Source: 8)

An Example of Cyber Resiliency

Let us illustrate this definition with an example. Suppose that Company XYZ has invested in all of the latest security technologies imaginable, but despite taking all of these safeguards, they are still hit with a large-scale cyberattack, such as that of ransomware.

Not many companies can withstand such an attack, and in most cases, they would most likely decide to go ahead and pay the money that is demanded from them so that they can resume mission-critical operations immediately.

But company ZYX decided not to go this route. They refused to pay the hacking group in question because they realized that if they did pay up, there is no guarantee that they will not be impacted again by the same Cyberattacker and asked for more money the second time around. In this regard, Company XYZ played their cards right, because they maintained a very proactive mindset.

With this, they created backups on a daily basis, and they also made use of a Cloud-based Infrastructure in which to host their entire IT and network infrastructure. Because of this, they were able to basically kill any of the virtual machines and the virtual desktops that were impacted by the ransomware, and within just a few hours, they were able to build new ones again and transfer all information and data to them from the backups.

So, within just a day or so, Company XYZ was back up on their feet running again, as if nothing had ever occurred. As it is legally required, the CISO of this company contacted all of the necessary law enforcement officials, notified key stake-holders of what had happened (especially their customers), and immediately launched a forensic investigation to determine what had exactly happened. The next mandate was to update all of the relevant security policies in order to reflect the lessons that have been learned from this incident.

How the Definition of Cyber Resiliency Was Met

So, as our illustration points out, Company XYZ met all of the components of Cyber resiliency, because they were able to:

- Greatly limit the impacts of the ransomware attack
- They were able to ensure its survival in just a matter of a day or two
- They are now prepared to mitigate the risk of the same threat vector (or for that matter, any of its variants) from happening again

So, cyber resiliency simply does not refer to how a business can just operate at *baseline levels* after being impacted. Rather, it refers to the fact as to how a business can resume operations back up to a *100%, normal speed* in the shortest time that is possible and reduce the chances of becoming a victim again.

What Is the Difference between Cyber Resiliency and Cyber Security?

There is often a great deal of confusion between the two, so here are the key differences:

Cyber security refers to the tools that are used to protect both digital and physical assets. So in the case of Company XYZ, this would include the routers, firewalls, network intrusion devices, proximity readers, key FOBS, etc. to protect the Intellectual Property (IP), the databases which contain the Personal Identifiable Information (PII) of both employees and customers, shared resources that are stored on the corporate servers, access to the secure rooms which contain actual client files, etc.

Cyber resiliency refers to how well Company XYZ can fully get into the mindset of a Cyberattacker in order to anticipate the new tools, as well as their elements of surprise in order to prevent them from penetrating into their lines of defenses and causing long-lasting damage.

In other words, Cyber security deals with the prevention of theft of information and data at just one point in time. Cyber resiliency is designed to protect the business from being permanently knocked off the grid over multiple periods of time. The former takes a pure technological approach, while the latter takes a much more psychological approach, which encompasses all facets of human behavior and culture at Company XYZ.

The NIST Special Publication 800-160 Volume 2

This bulletin (aka "Cyber Resiliency Considerations for the Engineering of Trustworthy Secure Systems") details the specific controls that a business must implement in order to come to an acceptable level of Cyber resiliency. This is provided in the matrix below:

The Control	It's Primary Objective
Adaptive Response	Have the ability and means to respond to a security breach in a quick and efficient manner
Analytic Monitoring	Be able to detect any anomalous or abnormal behavioral patterns quickly
Coordinated Projection	The need to implement multiple layers of authentication
Deception	Purposely confuse the Cyberattacker with regard to the main points of entry
Diversity	Use different kinds of techniques to further minimize the level of risk
Dynamic Positioning	Increase rapid recovery by further diversifying the main nodes of network communications distribution
Dynamic Representation	The importance of understanding the interlinkages between Cyber and non-Cyber resources
Nonpersistence	Keep resources only on an as-needed basis
Privilege Restriction	Assign only the appropriate permissions, rights, and accesses to employees to conduct their daily job functions
Realignment	Keep changing the interlinks so that a breakdown in noncritical assets will not have a cascading effect on the critical assets
Redundancy	Implement multiple instances of critical assets
Segmentation	Separate the network infrastructure into different subnets
Substantiated Integrity	Determine if critical assets have been further corrupted
Unpredictability	Keep mixing up your lines of defenses so that the Cyberattacker cannot plan their course of action

Data Loss

One of the biggest challenges for the CISO today is dealing with that of data leakages, whether they are intentional or not. In fact, this is one of the other "headache" areas for the CISO, which leads to their ultimate burnout. The next subsection goes into this in more detail.

The Data Breach

As a CISO, there is always a lot on your mind, on a constant, daily basis. These include delivering great customer service and keeping your products and services on the cutting edge as much as possible, in order to keep up with your competitors. But, there is yet another aspect that goes often overlooked: security. It's always on the back of your mind, but never really gets too much attention until you are actually impacted by a security breach.

Just consider some of these statistics for small businesses:

- A Cyberattack occurs every 39 seconds.
- One in three customers suffered some sort of data loss, out of a total of one billion accounts.
- It takes on average 191 days to detect that a malware attack has actually occurred.
- The top Cyberattacks for a small business (in order of prevalence) are Social Engineering, Insider Threats, and Advanced Persistent Threats.
- Only 14% of small business owners believe that they will be able to mitigate a Cyberattack.
- Only 39% of organizations actually keep their systems up to date with necessary software patches and upgrades.
- Only 51% of organizations actually have a dedicated budget for Cyber security.
- Over 60% of organizations will be *out of business just within six months* as a result of a Cyberattack.

- By the early next decade, Cyberattacks will cost organizations a staggering $6 trillion, and data breaches will cost $150 million.
- Each record of stolen data costs a small business owner $200.00.

Clearly, these numbers are very alarming, and as a small business owner, there is a lot that is stacked up against you. One could partly assume that this is due to a lack of financial resources, after all, you are on a tight budget. But, there are certain proactive steps that you can take, and these are detailed in the next section.

Top Five Tips to Avoid a Data Breach

1) *Collect only the needed information and data*

Obviously, when you start getting your client base established for your business, you will need to collect information and data about them. Some of this will include contact information (such as name, address, phone number, and possibly even credit card information). The database platform in which you store all of this should not only be secured but it is also important to *keep as much minimal data as possible.* For example, do you really need to store credit card information? True, this saves time for your customer, but if this financial data is stolen or compromised in any way, you will be held both *legally and financially responsible.* In fact, the average cost for a small business owner for such types of data loss is a staggering $280,000.00.

2) *Make sure the passwords that you establish are difficult to be broken by a Cyberattacker*

This is a topic that has been addressed in previous blogs, and yes, it still remains among one of the weakest links in the security chain for the small business owner. It is always important to make sure that your employees are on top of their game when it comes to creating strong passwords, and that they are not sharing it with anybody else. These standards need to be established in your security policies and firmly enforced. Also, consider very seriously using a password manager to help create and store long and complex passwords. Make use of implementing Two-Factor Authentication (2FA), in which more than one layer of security is used to protect your company data. A great tool for this is Biometrics, either Fingerprint or Iris Recognition.

3) *Make sure you use the proper levels of encryption*

This simply means that any communications (especially that of email) remains in a "garbled state" and stays that way until it is received by the legitimate party. This helps to ensure that if it were to be intercepted by a Cyberattacker, he or she will be unable to decipher it. Although this does not guarantee 100% security, the idea is that the Cyberattacker will get frustrated in the time that it actually takes to descramble the message and, as a result, will move onto a much less protected target.

4) *Limit network access*

For any business, large or small, the network component is at the heart of the IT infrastructure. After all, the servers reside here, from which your employees and other related personnel (such as outside vendors and contractors) can access information and data. Therefore, not only should you restrict the permissions in this regard but you need to make sure as well that all lines of communications between the servers, workstations, and wireless devices are secure. In this aspect, you should consider heavily using Virtual Private Networks (VPNs). Also, you need to know where all of this mission-critical information and data reside on your servers. Just consider some of these statistics:

a. Only 16% of small business owners know where their structured data resides at;

  b. Only 7% know the location of their unstructured data
     resides at.
5) *Not all Cyberattacks target electronic data*
     There is the misconception that only some kind of
  information is subject to an attack. But, keep in mind
  that there are also physical documents, which can also
  be a prime target, especially for an inside attack to occur.
  Therefore, make sure that the storage places within your
  business remain secure, with only those employees needing absolute access to it have the keys. Also, if you dis-
  pose of any paper documents, make sure that you shred
  them first. At the present time, there are no laws prevent-
  ing Dumpster Diving, and anybody can comb through
  your trash receptacles that are located outside. You may
  even want to consider outsourcing this function to a reputable paper-shredding company.

Internal Fraud Prevention

One of the hardest things for a CISO to do in their daily jobs
is to figure out where Internal Fraud could be precipitating at.
This is far unlike the threats coming in from the external environment, where the IT security team can get a clear view of
what is incoming. But the main problem with Internal Fraud
detection is that they are very often carried out by employees,
with whom the CISO could quite possibly have established
a solid working relationship. Thus, this makes it that much
harder to ascertain. The next subsection goes into this in
much more detail.

How to Avoid Internal Fraud

The goal of this is to fly under the radar for as long as
possible, as many businesses are simply not up to speed yet in
capturing these kinds of attacks.

But whatever variant it is, it all comes down to one thing: Fraud, especially that of internal ones, is extremely difficult to detect. The major reason for this is that they are often conducted by actual human beings, primarily carried out by using Social Engineering tactics.

For example, you could have an employee that you have had for a long period of time, they appear to be happy, but underneath, they are planning a Fraud-based attack on your company.

Employees, whether they have a criminal background or not, are often the most thought of suspect, because they know the internal workings of your organization, especially the weak spots. So it all comes down to one thing really, which is quite unfortunate in some ways:

You simply cannot trust anybody these days, no matter how well you may know them.

We will stick to how it relates to business and some measures you can take to help avoid it. Here we go:

1) *Create and deploy a fraud hotline*
   I have actually written about this before, but although employees might be the proverbial weakest link in the security chain, they can also be your best source of internal eyes. For example, depending upon how large your business is, you cannot be at all places all of the time. So, therefore, you have to rely on your employees to report anything to you that may be suspicious or simply out of the ordinary. Therefore, you need to maintain a special hotline in which an employee can anonymously report this kind of activity without any fear of reprisals being taken against them. In this regard, probably the best people to answer this hotline would be your IT security team. In fact, according to a recent report by the Association of Certified Fraud Examiners (also known as "ACFE"), 43% of all fraud cases are captured by these kinds of tips. More detail about this report can be found at this link:

https://www.acfeinsights.com/acfe-insights/announcing
-the-2020-report-to-the-nations.

But keep in mind one more important thing: All of
the above assumes that you still maintain a brick-and-
mortar office of sorts. Given how the world is now going
digital to the 99% Remote Workforce, obviously having
a tip line may not be as effective. Therefore, your best
bet is to migrate to a Cloud-based platform, such as that
of Microsoft Azure. They have all the tools you could
ever need to identify and stop fraudulent attacks on your
digital assets as they happen on a real-time basis. Heck,
they even give you tools to even help you track down the
perpetrator as well.

2) *Maintain the right set of controls*

Once again, this is one of the biggest buzzwords still
being bandied about in the world of Cybersecurity. But
you know what? Having the right set of controls in place
has now become mandatory, as set forth by the data
privacy laws of the GDPR and the CCPA, as well as others. The term controls is a catchall term, and which ones
you use are largely dependent upon the kind of digital
assets that you have. In terms of fraudulent-based activity, there are two types of controls: Active and passive.
With the former, it means that the controls you have in
place are doing their job to mitigate the risk of internal
fraud from actually happening. This would include setting up rights and permissions according to the job details
of the employee, having segregation of duties, deploying
Multifactor Authentication (MFA), having a regular password reset schedule, putting in physical devices to add
more security, etc. With the latter, as its name implies,
you are taking a less formal approach. Instead, you are
making use of audits, sudden changes in the level of
inventory, etc. in order to detect any fraudulent activity.
So you may be asking now which approach is the best?
Well, using both, and a hybrid approach is the best one

to take. This will help to ensure that you are taking all of the steps necessary to protect your business from internal fraud. In fact, according to the same report as just mentioned, almost 30% of all fraudulent activity occurs because of a sheer lack of controls.

3) *Watch for any signs of abnormalities*

Let's face it, life is a rat race. We all have our daily ups and downs and emotional swings. It is just a part of who we are as human beings. But one thing for sure is that no matter how much we try to hide our feelings and emotions so that they are not so apparent to others, there are always involuntary clues that are given out. But when it comes to your employees, one of the key things to look out for is how their behavior changes when they do, they work. For example, if there are drastic mood swings, unusual relationships with external, third parties, a reluctance to attend meetings, or even share responsibilities, these are for sure red flags. Now it doesn't necessarily mean that your employee who is displaying these emotions is going to launch an internal fraud attack, but typically it is those that are disgruntled are more prone to doing this.

Identity and Access Management

The CISO is now starting to realize that whatever authentication mechanisms are currently in place is that it is not enough to truly ascertain the identity of a particular individual. Another nightmare issue in dealing with this is how to come up with the best framework possible so that it becomes not only harder for the Cyberattacker to break through but also guarantee the identity of the employees that are logging in in order to gain access to the shared resources. This is even more critical now as the Remote Workforce is now taking a permanent hold in Corporate America. One of these is the adoption of the Zero Trust Framework, which is also reviewed in more detail.

The next subsections go into this much more in detail.

Biometrics and Identity Management

Introduction

As we are now into the start of 2022, many of the Cybersecurity pundits have already made their predictions as to what the Threat Landscape will look like. While some have predicted gloom and doom scenarios, others believe that it will be the same as 2019, but only slightly worse.

But there seems to be one common thread with all of these predictions: Despite passwords being the weakest link in the security chain, they will still be the de facto standard that will be used in terms of Identity Management and authenticating end users.

Because of this, the password will still be a highly sought-after item for the Cyberattacker. In a way, this is becoming a cat-and-mouse game. Businesses understand the need to create long and complex passwords, but to employees, they are too difficult to remember. As a result, they resort back to using passwords that can be easily hacked into (such as using "password", or "123456").

What can be done to alleviate this issue? There are some options out there, which include the use of Password Managers. These are software applications that can create and store these long and complex passwords, as well as using Biometric Technology, which is the focal point of this chapter.

What Biometrics Is All About

Biometrics has actually been around for quite a long time, going all the way back to the 1960s. But it is only now that it has started to make its splash in the realm of Identity

Management. You may be wondering what it is all about? Biometrics is simply another way of confirming the identity of an end user via their unique physiological and behavioral traits. This includes the following:

- Your fingerprint (such as the ridges, whorls, and valleys that are found within it)
- Your hand (this includes the shape of the hand and the geometric distances between the features of it)
- Your eye (this encompasses both the iris and the retina – the former is the colored region between the pupil and the sclera, and the latter refers to groups of blood vessels in the back)
- Your face (this includes the examination of your lips, nose, chin, eyebrows, etc. and the corresponding distances between them)
- Your voice (this is the differing voice inflections in our everyday speech)
- Your signature (note that this is not the signature itself, but in the mannerisms in which we sign our name)
- Your keystroke (these are the mannerisms in which we type on our computer or wireless device keyboard)

The first five are known as "Physical Biometrics", and the last two are known as "Behavioral Biometrics".

(Source: https://www.fbi.gov/services/cjis/ fingerprints-and-other-biometrics/biometric-center-of -excellence/modalities)

How Biometrics Can Confirm Your Identity

Biometrics can be installed in many types of configurations, from being very complex to very simple. Probably the best example of this is the TouchID and FaceID that are used in the latest versions of the iPhone. But no matter what the configuration is, there is a methodology that is used across all the Biometric modalities in order to confirm the identity of an individual which is as follows:

- Raw pictures and/or samples are collected and converted into various images.
- These images are then combined into one master image.
- From the master image, the unique images are then extracted and evaluated by the Biometric system.
- Once the unique features have been extracted, they are then converted over into a unique mathematical file; this becomes known as the "Enrollment Template" and is permanently stored into the database of the Biometric system.
- If an end user wishes to gain either physical or logical access entry, he or she must go through the first three steps again. The end result is that the "Verification Template" is thus created.
- The Enrollment and Verification Templates are then compared against one another to determine the statistical closeness between the two. If there is a close enough match between the two, the end user is then granted access to the resource that he or she is seeking. If there is not enough closeness, then the individual must start this entire process all over again, from the very beginning.

   It is important to note that the first three steps are known as the "Enrollment Phase", and the last two are known as the "Verification Phase".

(Source: https://www.researchgate.net/figure/ Enrollment-verification-identification-in-a-biometric -system_fig4_260684432)

Biometrics as a Replacement to the Password

As previously mentioned, using a password manager is a good option to have in order to enforce your Identity Management

Policies. But what about something even better? Well, there is Biometrics. This technology is fast becoming seen as the ultimate replacement to the password.

When Biometrics is used in this regard, it is known as a "Single Sign Solution", or an "SSO" for short. The reason why it is called so is that in literally one scan of your fingerprint or iris, you can be logged into a computer or wireless device in just a matter of a few seconds.

Although in theory any Biometric modality can be used as an SSO, it is primarily that of Fingerprint Recognition and Iris Recognition that are being used across Corporate America, whether it is an SMB or even a Fortune 100 company. Facial Recognition is starting to be used, but there are still issues, especially with those related to privacy rights.

This Fingerprint Recognition device can be installed directly onto your workstation with a USB cable. The red portion on top is the optical sensor from which an end user places their fingerprint and where both the Enrollment and Verification processes take place. All that is needed is the appropriate driver which can be downloaded in just a matter of a few minutes. In this regard, Fingerprint Recognition is deemed to be a "full contact" type of technology, in that the end user has to have physical contact with the device.

This kind of device works exactly in the same manner as the Fingerprint Recognition device as seen previously. But the only difference is that this is a "non-contact" kind of technology, in that all the end user has to do is merely point the camera (which is the large circle at the top of the device) in front of their eye at reasonably close proximity so that a good quality image of the iris can be captured.

It is important to note that both of these devices illustrated are external devices; in many computers and wireless devices today, these kinds of cameras and sensors are actually embedded into the hardware themselves.

There are a number of key advantages as to why organizations should seriously consider adopting Biometric-based SSOs versus using the traditional password as the primary means of confirming the identity of an individual:

- Unlike passwords, your fingerprint or iris cannot be stolen, they are a permanent part of you.
- Just about every human being on the planet has their own unique set of fingerprints or irises – therefore, they cannot be replicated, unlike a password.
- Because the Enrollment and Verification Templates are actual mathematical files, there is nothing that a Cyberattacker can do with them in the case that they are hijacked, unlike with stolen passwords or credit card numbers.
- It is quite difficult to reverse engineer these mathematical files in order to construct the original composite images of either the fingerprint or the iris.
- An end user can literally be logged into their workstation or wireless device in just a matter of a few seconds, versus the minutes it can take to use a password. Although this time gap may not appear to be too significant, the time savings can add up in the long term, and thus result in greater employee productivity.
- In most businesses, the typical administrative cost to reset a password is about $400 per year per employee. A Biometrics-based SSO totally eradicates this cost.
- Because employees will no longer have to remember long and complex passwords, the so-called "Post It Syndrome" is also totally eliminated. This is the situation where the employee writes down their password and sticks it at their workstation monitor so that they can remember it more easily.
- As mentioned, since everybody has a unique fingerprint and iris structure, by using them as an SSO, the overall security posture of a business is further enhanced because passwords are no longer needed and thus not being used.

■ Fraud is also becoming a huge and escalating reality, but using Biometrics-based SSOs should help to bring these levels down drastically because, after all, nobody can replicate your fingerprint or iris.

An Introduction to the Zero Trust Framework

Introduction

As we see the number of COVID-19 cases spike upward almost completely out of control, the concept of the Remote Workforce is going to be around for a long time to come, most likely even into early 2022.

With this in mind, many businesses across Corporate America are now thoroughly assessing and taking stock of what they can do to protect probably their most confidential and prized digital asset – the databases that house the Personal Identifiable Information of both employees and customers.

Since the Cyberattacker is always coming up with new ways in which to tap into it – very often in a covet fashion without you knowing about it until it is too late to do anything about it. What can be done about this? This is where the Zero Trust Framework comes into play and is the focal point in this article.

What Exactly Is Zero Trust?

Zero Trust is not a brand-new Cybersecurity technology, nor is it a product or service. Instead, it is a concept that has its roots in what is known as the "Principle of Least Privilege", also known simply as "PoLP".

This merely states that an end user should not be given any more rights, accesses, and privileges to shared resources than what is absolutely necessary in order for that individual to conduct their daily job responsibilities. But with this, there is an implied or implicit baseline of trust that is given.

But with Zero Trust, it takes this principle to yet another extreme in which nobody at all is trusted in both the internal and the external environments of your company. In other words, it is not just the end users, but even devices and other end-user profiles cannot be trusted at all. In order to gain access to what is needed, all of these entities must be fully vetted and authenticated to the maximum level possible.

In this regard, even using Two-Factor Authentication (2FA) is simply not enough. The use of Multifactor Authentication (MFA) is required, in which at least three layers (preferably even more) are used in order to 100% fully verify the device or the end user in question.

In fact, a key distinction with the Zero Trust Framework is that it is not typically used for just enhancing the primary lines of defense for the business. Rather, this new way of thinking in Cybersecurity is further extended to protect *each and every* server, workstation, and other assets that reside within the IT infrastructure.

Although as just mentioned, making use of MFA is highly favored, and other items can be used as well in order to fully enforce the Zero Trust Framework, which are as follows:

- Implementing stronger levels of Endpoint Security
- Breaking up your entire Network infrastructure into smaller segments, which are known as "Subnets"
- Identity and Access Management (IAM)
- Role-Based Access Control (RBAC)
- Deploying very high levels of encryption
- Logging and analytic tools
- Making use of Policy Enforcement and Orchestration Engines

How to Implement the Zero Trust Framework

It is important to keep in mind that deploying Zero Trust is not something that happens in just one fell swoop; rather, it is implemented in stages, using a phased-in approach. The following are key areas that you need to keep in mind as you deploy it:

1) *Understand and completely define what needs to be protected*

    With Zero Trust, you don't assume that your most vulnerable digital assets are at risk. Rather, you take the position that everything is prone to a security breach, no matter how minimal it might be to your company. In this regard, you are taking a much more holistic view, in that you are not simply protecting what you think the different potential attack planes could be, but you are viewing this as an entire surface that needs 100% protection, on a 24 × 7 × 365 basis. So, you and your IT security team need to take a very careful inventory of everything digital that your company has, and from there, map out how each of them will be protected. So rather than having the mindset of one overall arching line of defense for your business, you are now taking the approach of creating many different "Micro Perimeters" for each individual asset.

2) *Determine the interconnections*

    In today's environment, your digital assets are not just isolated to themselves. For example, your primary database will be connected with others, as well as to other servers, which are both physical and virtual in nature. Because of this, you also need to ascertain how these linkages work with another, and from there, determine the types of controls that can be implemented in between these digital assets so that they can be protected.

3) *Crafting the Zero Trust Framework*

    It is important to keep in mind instituting this does not take a "one-size-fits-all" approach. Meaning, what may work for one company will not work for your business. The primary reason for this is that not only do you have your own unique set of security requirements, but the protection surface (as defined in Step #1) and the linkages that you have determined (defined in Step #2) will also be unique to you. Therefore, you need to take the mindset that you need to create your framework as to what your needs are at that moment in time, as well as considering projected future needs.

4) *Drafting the Security Policies*

Once you have determined how your overall Zero Trust Framework will look like, you then need to create the Security Policies that will go along with it. For example, it will be very detailed and granular in nature, given the "Micro Perimeters" approach that the Zero Trust uses. So, you will need to determine the following for each and every digital asset that you have mapped out (which was accomplished in Step #1):

a. Who the end users are (this will be your employees, contractors, outside third-party vendors and suppliers, etc.);

b. The types of shared resources that they will be accessing on a daily basis;

c. What those specific access mechanisms will be;

d. The security mechanisms (particularly the controls) that will be used to protect that level of access.

5) *Implement how the Zero Trust Framework will be determined*

Once you have accomplished steps #1-#4, the final goal to be achieved is how it will be monitored on a real-time basis. In this particular instance, you will want to make use of what is known as a Security Information and Event Management (SIEM) software package. This is an easy to deploy tool that will collect all of the logging and activity information, as well as all of the warnings and alerts, and put them into one central view. The main advantage of this is that your IT security team will be able to triage and act upon those threat variants almost instantaneously.

The Advantages of the Zero Trust Framework

These are as follows:

1) *A much greater level of accountability*

   When the Remote Workforce started to take full swing last year because of COVID-19, many companies were in a rush to issue company devices. Unfortunately, not every business entity could do this, and as a result of this, employees were forced to use their own devices in order to conduct their daily job tasks. But this also triggered a whole new host of security issues. But as organizations are starting to implement the concept of Zero Trust, there is now a much higher degree of accountability of which devices are being used for in this regard. For example, if an employee wishes to gain access to corporate resources on their own device, they can no longer do so, as they now must use company-issued equipment which possess these authentication mechanisms so that access can be granted.

2) *It facilitates the use of centralized monitoring*

   When security tools and technologies are used in different combinations with no planning in mind, it can be very difficult for the IT security team to keep track of all of the warnings and alerts that are coming in. This can make it very difficult to triage and escalate the real Cyber threats that are out there. But with the Zero Trust methodology, since each and every device is accounted for in a logical manner, a centralized approach can now be utilized. One typical example of this is what is known as the Security Incident and Event Management software application. With this, not only can the false positives be filtered by making use of both Artificial Intelligence (AI) and Machine Learning (ML) but the legitimate warnings and alerts can be presented on a real-time basis through a centralized dashboard. Thus, this allows the IT security team to be far more proactive, and in turn, greatly reduce the response times to combating the various threat vectors.

3) *Almost total elimination of passwords*

The password has long been the de facto standard in order to authenticate an individual to gain access to shared resources. But even despite the advancements of Password Managers, people are still stuck in their old ways, making passwords even more vulnerable than they were ever before. With the Zero Trust Framework, much greater efforts are now taken to totally eradicate the use of passwords and use much more robust authentication tools. For example, there is now a heavy reliance upon using Biometric Technology. With this, a unique physiological or behavioral trait is extracted from the individual in order to 100% confirm their identity, which obviously nobody else possesses. The biggest advantage of this is that different kinds and types of Biometric modalities (such as Fingerprint Recognition, Iris Recognition, Facial Recognition, etc.) can be implemented at different points in the corresponding security layers. For example, they can be used individually, and in tandem with each other to create a very secure environment.

4) *Scalability is offered*

With the Remote Workforce now guaranteed to be a long-term phenomenon, many companies are now opting to make greater usage of Cloud-based resources, such as those offered by the AWS or Microsoft Azure. There are of course those entities that still choose to have a brick-and-mortar presence, and to a certain degree, still have some remnants of an On-Premises solution. But whatever option is chosen, the Zero Trust Framework allows for the seamless transfer for apps, digital assets, and even the confidential information and data (especially the Personal Identifiable Information [PII] datasets) from one place to another in a much more secure fashion.

5) *Breaking in becomes close to impossible*

Before the COVID-19 pandemic hit, many businesses adopted what is known as the "Perimeter Security" approach to protecting their digital assets. This simply means that there was only one line of defense separating the internal environment from the external environment. As a result, if the Cyberattacker were to penetrate through this, they could gain access to just about anything in the IT and network infrastructure and move covertly in a lateral fashion. But with the Zero Trust Framework, the implementation of multiple layers of security means that it becomes that much harder for the Cyberattacker to gain access to the proverbial "Crown Jewels", as it will take much longer to break through each and every line of defense, as they try to go deeper in. In the end, more than likely, he or she will just give up.

6) *Greater adherence to compliance*

With the heightened enforcement of the GDPR, CCPA, HIPAA, etc. companies now have to come into compliance with all of the various statutes and provisions that are applicable to them. By adopting the Zero Trust Framework, businesses will now be assured of keeping up that level of compliance, as they will be forced now to implement the right set of controls (which are essentially the authentication mechanisms) in order to protect their PII datasets, which is what is being scrutinized the most by auditors and regulators.

Third-Party and Vendor Risk Management

Making the CISO even more ill today is the thought of having to deal with the responsibility of outside, external third parties that their company has to work with. From the standpoint of Cybersecurity, the CISO is ultimately responsible for making sure that the security policies and protocols that are in place at the third party closely match their own. Also, if there are any security breaches that happen to the PII datasets that the external, third party has been entrusted with, the CISO is also responsible for this, and could even be held personally liable for this. The following subsections examine this in more detail.

How to Manage Third-Party Risk

Introduction

To some degree or another, most businesses rely upon other third parties in order to carry out their necessary business functions. Depending upon what your enterprise is in, this could be simply staff augmentation or purchasing raw materials in order to manufacture the products or create the services that your customers require.

Whatever it is, the days of having an implicit level of trust are over, largely due to the impacts of the COVID-19 pandemic. Now, you have to vet your third parties just as much (or perhaps even more) as you would when hiring new employees. This is the focal point of this article.

The Types of Third-Party Risks

At the present time, when one hears the term "risk", the thoughts of Cybersecurity threats from your third party transmitted down to your business very often come to mind. But keep in mind, there are other types of third-party risks that can be just as lethal to your business. Some of these include the following:

1) *Brand risk*
    This is also commonly referred to as "Reputational Risk". This occurs when your third party has received any sort of negative attention, in news headlines or other forms of media outlets.

2) *Process (Operational) risk*

This happens when a mission-critical process breaks down for a period of time at the location of your third party. This can greatly impact your supply chain and put a serious cringe on product/service delivery to your customers.

3) *Disaster Recovery risk*

In the event that your third party experiences a massive Cyberattack or other types of natural disaster, this could also have a severe impact on your own business. Thus, it is important that they have not only a solid Disaster Recovery (DR) plan in place but a Business Continuity (BC) plan as well in order to prove their level of "Cyber Resiliency" to you (this merely refers to how quickly they can bounce back from a security breach).

4) *Data privacy risk*

This is probably one of the biggest areas of concern at the present time. For example, there are good chances that you will be sharing confidential information (especially as it relates to your customers) with your third party. Just as much as you are vigilant in protecting, you have to make sure of this with them as well. If there are any security breaches that occur with your third party which involves the loss or malicious heisting of information/data, you will be held responsible, not them. This issue has become much more prevalent with the recent passages of the CCPA and the GDPR.

5) *Noncompliance risk*

Just as much as you have to be compliant with the recent regulatory frameworks, so does the third party that you onboard. If they are not, there are good chances that they could be audited, and your business could also be dragged into it.

6) *Credit (financial) risk*

This kind of risk can also be of grave concern, especially during this time of lockdowns. If your third party does not have enough cash flow or reserves on hand to sustain themselves during this pandemic, you should act quickly in order to find another suitable one that can deliver your needs right on time, without any disruptions to your own processes.

7) *Geopolitical risk*

This typically happens when your third party is located in an entirely different country. For instance, various political events could rock your supply chain, or even Insider Attacks can damage the parts that you need in order to produce and deliver a quality product.

How to Manage Third-Party Risks

There are numerous steps that you can take to mitigate your level of risk to the third parties that you hire, which include:

■ *Hire a dedicated individual*

Being a member of the C-Suite or even the business owner, your time is obviously at a premium. Therefore, you should hire somebody whose sole job is to locate and vet out possible third-party vendors as your company needs them. Probably one of the biggest qualifications that you should require of him or her is their ability to take a close look at the security policies and the respective level of enforcement at the third party you are looking at hiring. Also, they should be able to carefully examine just how well they protect their own confidential information/data, as this will be a reflection as to how they will treat the ones that belong to your organization.

■ *Launch a very detailed due diligence process*

By this, you are literally conducting a background check on the third party you are planning to hire. For example, not only should you examine their financial stability and brand reputation but you also need to pay very careful attention as it relates to Cybersecurity. For example, you need to make sure that their practices and policies mesh up to the high standards that you have set forth for your own company. Not only this, but to a certain degree, your dedicated third-party manager should be allowed to examine just how well the lines of defenses are fortified at your potential third party, as it relates to their IT and network infrastructures. Keep in mind that any security breach that impacts them could also hit you, as the Cyberattacker will be on the lookout for these kinds of business relationships.

■ *Create an ironclad contract*

Before you actually hire a third party, you must have a contract in place that spells out in detail the responsibilities that the third party has to you, and this has to be enforceable at any time. For instance, if you suspect that there could be a lack of enforcement as it relates to internal controls, then you should have the right to inspect that and recommend a corrective course of action that should be implemented ASAP. Also, the contract should stipulate that you can conduct an audit any time that is deemed necessary in order to make sure that your third party is living up to its end of the obligations.

The Importance of Vendor Compliance Management

Introduction

In today's world of commerce, there are many links that exist between companies all over the world. Probably one of the best examples is the suppliers and other external, third parties that you rely on.

For instance, if you manufacture products and distribute them onto the marketplace, you will be dependent upon other entities to provide you with the raw materials, as well others in order to ensure that what you deliver to your customers is of high caliber.

But with all these interconnections, any failure at one node can have a fast, cascading effect on other parts of your manufacturing and distribution processes. One area in which this can happen is Cybersecurity and is the focal point of this article.

What Is Vendor Compliance?

Simply put, it can be specifically defined as follows:

> It refers to managing all aspects of your company's and your suppliers' compliance with statutory, legal, and technical requirements. It ensures both your business and your suppliers are legally compliant, vetted, and verified to access industry-relevant trading opportunities and mitigate trading risks.

(Source: 9)

In other words, you want the third parties that you rely upon to be up to the same Cybersecurity standards that you have established and maintained for your business. This includes primarily two areas:

- The protection of Personal Identifiable Information (PII) datasets
- Compliance with the recent data privacy laws, especially those of the CCPA and the GDPR

In most instances, you will be sharing confidential data about your customers to these vendors in order to accomplish the tasks that you have outsourced to them. You must completely ensure that all security protocols are in place (like how you have them) to protect your customers, especially when it comes from the standpoint of authentication. For example, only those individuals that must access it will have their identity confirmed across different levels.

Also, you have to make sure that these third parties are also in full compliance with the regulatory statutes as just described. The bottom line is that if any of the PII datasets that you have trusted to your third party is released either accidentally or maliciously, you will be at fault for this, not them. You will be the one facing the audits and the potential harsh financial penalties that are imposed by the data privacy laws, not them.

Therefore, you need to take the time to carefully scrutinize each vendor you consider. You must have a reliable and comprehensive vetting process in place before you decide on an external, third party that you can work with. This is where the role of having a good Vendor Compliance Program will come into crucial play.

The Components

When it comes to Cybersecurity, creating a Vendor Compliance Program can also be referred to as the "Vendor Cyber Risk Management Framework", or "VCRMF" for short. It should include the following:

1) *Implement a well-known model*

True, you can pretty much set up your own checklist in deciding what you need to look for when deciding upon hiring a third party to work with. But if this is the first time that you are doing this, it is highly recommended that you make use of an already established template in order to fully ensure that you have all your bases covered. One such highly regarded methodology that you can make use of is known as the "NIST Cybersecurity Framework". More information about this can be downloaded here. The models that are provided by NIST already have a listing of standards and best practices that you start using almost immediately. They also have an established list of security controls and risk management tools that you can implement not only for your own

business but for your hired third party as well. A key
certification that you need to make sure that your potential third-party vendor has is what is known as the "ISO
27001". If they have this designation, then you can be
assured that they already have a strong set of controls and
procedures in place to safeguard their own PII datasets. It
simply means that the PII datasets that you hand over to
them will be as secure as possible.

2) *Making sure of compliance*

As you start to craft out your VCRMF, it is absolutely critical that you have a section on it in which you check that
your potential third party has achieved a full level of compliance in your specific industry. For instance, if you are a
health-care organization, they will be bound not only to the
policies of the GDPR and the CCPA but also to HIPAA. A
good way to initiate this process is by making a detailed list
of the Cyber-related checks and balances that you have and
cross comparing that with what the third party that you are
considering hiring also has in place. If there are any gap-
ing discrepancies, then you know it is time to move on and
start looking for a new partner to work with. Also, in this
vetting process, you also need to find out if they have been
the subject of any audits and/or fines. If there are any, then
this should also be a red flag to you.

3) *It is not a one and done process*

Many businesses think that once they have carefully
screened and thoroughly vetted out their external, third
parties from the outset, then all the work is done. But
this is not the case at all. During the relationships you
have established, the working dynamics can always
change, especially from the standpoint of Cybersecurity.
Therefore, you need to make sure that the process you
have set forth to make sure that your third parties are in
the levels of compliance that you expect them to be at
is an iterative one. This simply means that you have the
right to execute random audits on them to make sure that

the same security protocols and controls are still in place as when you first hired them. A key point to remember here is that the terms for carrying out this kind of audit should be explicitly spelled out in the contract that you sign with them, just to avoid any potential misunderstandings down the road. In fact, according to a recent study by Garner, 83% of all Cybersecurity risks escalate after the contract has been signed and the work has been started.

Also, clear lines of communications must be in place as the relationship develops with your third-party vendor. For example, if they have been hit by a Cyberattack, they must notify you immediately so that you can take steps to mitigate the risks of this happening to your business.

Investigations and Forensics

Another area that is quite stressful for the CISO (and leading to the burnout rate) is that they are tasked with the primary responsibility of launching and conducting the Forensics Investigation after they have been impacted by a Cyberattack. Law enforcement wants everything down now so that they can have the evidence at hand to bring to justice the Cyberattacker that was responsible. But unfortunately, conducting a detailed Forensics-based exam takes a lot of time, and the CISO has to balance this out with the unrealistic demands of law enforcement. The next subsection examines this in more detail.

The Use of Artificial Intelligence in Digital Forensics

As we steamroll into 2022, one of the biggest buzzwords being spoken of is Artificial Intelligence, or AI for short. Essentially, the concept of this mimics the thought and reasoning processes of the human brain and applies that to help streamline and/or automate manual processes.

AI is starting to find its role in Cybersecurity, especially as it relates to filtering for false positives and taking manual tasks deemed time-consuming.

It is also finding a strong foothold in the world of Digital Forensics. In this chapter, we review some real-world uses of AI.

How It Is Being Used

1) *It is being used for data collection*

   Whenever a Digital Forensics team conducts an investigation, every effort is taken to make sure that all pieces of evidence are collected to a pre-established set of best standards and practices so that they can be admissible in a court of law. But the problem is that if there is a lot of evidence, the information and data associated with them will have to be condensed to some degree or another so that it can be transmitted to the other parties involved for analysis purposes. This can be a very time-consuming and laborious process to take on for any human being, which can be well spent on other more pressing issues. This is where AI can come in. Not only can it compress them down in a short period of time but, better yet, it can also do a deeper dive into the analysis of the information and data and even discover hidden correlations that the human eye cannot pick up even after a few glances.

2) *It can prepare the needed databases*

   Whenever the evidence is collected from the crime scene, one of the first tasks is to create the databases that will store them. Traditionally, this task has been left to somebody on the Digital Forensics team to handle. While that particular individual is probably very good at doing it, keep in mind that human beings are prone to error. Thus, when these databases are created, they have to be as airtight as possible so that there is no data leakage, whether it is intentional or not. Based on the rules and mathematical algorithms that you feed into your AI tool, not only can the creation of these databases be automated but they will also be created with the highest security levels in mind. As an added bonus, the AI system can also quickly configure and deploy those rights, permissions, and privileges needed for only authorized individuals allowed to access the evidence. Even better, if it detects any unauthorized access attempt, you will be notified immediately.

3) *The embracing of the IoT*

Most of us have heard of this acronym before, and it stands for the "Internet of Things"." This is where all of the objects we interact with in both the physical and virtual worlds are connected. Some examples of this are Siri and Cortana, the Virtual Personal Assistants (VPAs), found on both iOS and Windows, respectively. Another is that of the Smart Home. This is where at the clap of your hands, you can either turn on your TV or even start brewing your cup of coffee. The same holds true for the world of Digital Forensics. Every part of the investigative and evidence presentation process is now interlinked, driven primarily by IoT. For example, AI can closely examine the structure of a raw image taken by a camera and link that to other pieces of evidence, such as content found in an email message or Social Media posting. Better yet, it can even describe the degree of that correlation and even provide recommendations as to how it can be best showcased in a court of law. It can also take even newer pieces of evidence and correlate that with older pieces that have been collected previously. Even criminal records can be matched up as well.

4) *It is useful for "What If Scenarios"*

Some of the digital evidence collected from a crime scene may not prove to be as useful as others. But the bottom line is that in order to build a solid case, all pieces must be somehow used, even if they have the remotest of uses. This is where the role of constructing hypothetical situations can come into play. AI can help to build robust "What-If

Scenarios" from these less useful pieces of evidence and show other forms of intent that the criminal could have embarked on as well. In other words, AI can take hunches and gut feelings that cannot be explained easily and transform them into real-world, believable scenarios.

5) *It is excellent for Data Mining*

As it was mentioned earlier in this blog, AI can be used to help discover hidden trends in the pieces of evidence that are collected. But better yet, AI knows no bounds to how much data it can process and analyze. For example, it can go through Terabytes and even Petabytes of information and data in just a matter of a few minutes to find even much deeper trends and correlations in the datasets. This is also known as "Data Mining"," or "Big Data"." In this regard, a subset of AI, known as "Machine Learning" ("ML"), is used, as it can be used for incorporating highly complex statistical principles into the Data Mining process.

Governance

Finally, as mentioned throughout this chapter, the CISO is ultimately responsible for the safety and security of all of the physical and digital assets. If anything happens, they are the first who get to be blamed. The following subsection examines this in more detail.

Understanding IT Governance, Risk, and Compliance

Introduction

In the world of Cybersecurity, there is no shortage of buzz words and technojargon. Many times many of them are used together, causing even more confusion. One such grouping of these words is Governance, Risk, and Compliance. While a business needs all three of these to work together in a seamless fashion, they do have different purposes as well.

What Exactly Do They Mean?

The definitions for these terms can be broken down as follows:

1) *Governance*

As it relates to IT, this is how an organization is run. Typically, this will be from a top-down structure. For example, at the top is the CISO, beneath him or her would be the managers from the IT department and the IT security team, followed then by the Project Managers who are responsible for managing the employees that are getting the deliverables done for the client. A typical example of this would be a software development team. The developers report to the Project Manager, who then would report to the Department Manager. The characteristics of an effective chain of command in this regard exhibits the following:

a. A clear and transparent line of communication: The vision, the goals, and the objectives must be transmitted all the down to the lowest-ranking IT member, and likewise, the needs and ideas of the IT security team must be heard and listened to and transmitted back to the CISO for evaluation to see if the money can be appropriated.

b. Effective resource allocation: The CISO and the respective managers work together as a cohesive unit in order to distribute scarce resources in order to effectively manage the Cyber Threat Landscape as best as possible.

c. A system of checks and balances: The CISO and his or her top-level managers must enforce the divisional lines of who is responsible for what and must also make sure that there is a strong sense of accountability.

    d. Rewards/acknowledgments: A good Governance system will reward those employees who have made an impact in protecting the digital assets of the company, as well as those who have maintained a good level of Cyber Hygiene. Likewise, rather than singling out and punishing those employees who may have made a mistake, constructive criticism will instead be offered.

2) *Compliance*

This is when your company has policies and rules that abide by the security requirements of other entities that you deal with. Probably the best examples of this are data privacy, most notably those of the GDPR and the CCPA. They have provisions and mandates that you must meet in order to safeguard primarily the Personal Identifiable Information (PII) datasets that you have been entrusted with. Characteristics of a good Compliance program include:

    a. Choosing the right framework(s) or methodologies: This will guide you in the process of selecting the best controls possible to protect confidential information and data.

    b. Having a change management system in place: Any adjustments or changes that you make to the controls are well documented, and any upgrades or new tools/technologies that are to be deployed are first tested in a controlled environment before being released to production status.

3) *Risk*

This typically refers to the amount of "pain" your company can withstand before a threat variant makes permanent damage to your IT and network infrastructure. There are other sorts of definitions and ways to calculate risk, but some of the common traits of a good Risk Management program are as follows:

a. A categorization scheme has been created: With this, you are taking an inventory of all your digital assets, and in turn, deciding (based upon both quantitative and qualitative factors) which are most prone, and least suspect to an impact if your organization becomes a victim of a security breach. For example, the database that houses the PII datasets would be a prime target and thus will need the most amount of controls in order to protect it. Because of this, it will receive a numerical ranking of 10 (where 10 would be most vulnerable and 1 would be least vulnerable on the categorization scale). Whereas, the documented minutes from meetings held a long time ago will most likely not be a highly sought-after target; therefore, they will only need a minimal amount of controls, if any, thus giving them a ranking of about 3.

b. The controls are monitored: Just like the other components of your IT and network infrastructure, Risk Controls can go stale and lose their effectiveness if they are not kept up to date with the latest patches and upgrades. Therefore, a good Risk Management program will keep an eye on all of your controls on a real-time basis, and alert you and your IT security team if any of them need further attention and/or optimization.

Other Factors That Keep the CISO Up at Night

The previous subsection reviewed in extensive detail what some of the major roles and duties of a CISO are. There is no doubt that it is quite expansive, and the responsibilities are only going to get greater as the Cybersecurity Threat

Landscape keeps changing in both the short and long terms. Even with the list reviewed, it is still too much for any one individual to handle on their own. That is one of the primary reasons why the burnout of the CISO is so high these days.

But there are other factors at play here as well, and these include the following, which are reviewed.

1) *Strategic Alignment*

    The CISO must work to their specific strategies with both the mission of the business and the C-Suite so that its goals and tolerance for risk are assessed properly.

2) *Changing Regulations*

    There has been an explosion in the data privacy laws both on the national level and on the international level. These change quite frequently as the United States Congress and governments worldwide pass legislation and new threats emerge. In the wake of the GDPR, more governments at all levels are following the exact same format of it, which means the standards for information security compliance will continue to become more complex.

3) *Cloud Security*

    As businesses in Corporate America moved their On-Premises Infrastructure to the Cloud (such as that of the AWS and Microsoft Azure), the CISO is charged with improving the security, identity, and access management across the entire realms of public and private Cloud-based environments. At the same time, the security of on-premises legacy systems must be maintained, if the businesses maintain that sort of Hybrid-based environment.

4) *Team Development*

    The utilities industry here in the United States claims that there are fewer than 500 people in the United States with the necessary cybersecurity training in this area. Plus, only 15% of CISOs plan to stay in their current roles from within this industry. With the average tenure of a

CISO being just two to three years, a CISO must be an engaging and dynamic leader that responds to employees' needs. Equally important is the encouragement of their career growth in order to drive down attrition.

5) *Emerging Technology*

CISOs must also keep up with Cyber-based technology trends, and they must stay vigilant and be proactive to take advantage of emerging tools, which include the following:

a. Artificial Intelligence (AI)
b. Machine Learning (ML)
c. The Internet of Things (IoT)
d. The advent of 5G wireless-based networks
e. Newer cloud-based security products and services enable IT Security teams to multiple detect threats variants

6) *Data Management*

With this being at the top of the priority list, the CISO on a daily basis must seek out stronger data governance practices. Also, the CISO must keep assessing and cleanse all of the datasets that their company makes use of.

7) *Incident Response and Remediation*

Perhaps most challenging of all, the CISO, must face the new reality: data breaches and leakages. Thus, the CISO needs to address the potential risk brought on by digital transformation and the use of third-party vendors.

8) *The CISO often is too technical that focuses exclusively on the nuts and bolts of security*

The CISO is often blamed to focus much more heavily on solving security issues rather than also focusing on risk management as part of the larger business strategy.

9) *The CISO lacks training in traditional business skills*

Along with the other roles in the C-Suite, technical knowledge is not the only skill required to win at the job. As a result, gaining executive buy-in for initiative adoption requires the CISO to create collaborative bridges with other business units.

What the CISO Can Do to Improve the Odds of Tenure

As mentioned earlier in this chapter, the average tenure rate for a CISO is at two years before they burn out, quit, or get terminated. But if he or she wants to stay longer at the job, what can they do? Here are a few pointers:

1) *Improve the lines of communication and foster a shared, collaborative environment*

   This can be achieved with the following:

   a. Communicate technical information to nontechnical speak so that everybody in the company can understand it

   b. Implement information in terms of business outcomes, and not just quantitative-based measures

   c. Build strategic alliances with other C-level executives to get their buy-in in order to change the conversation from constantly "putting out fires" to growing and transforming the business proactively

   d. Align security strategies with business opportunities and goals of the company

   e. Adopt a broader risk management strategy instead of getting bogged down with minor details

2) *Understand the true needs of the business*

   a. Become acclimated with the everyday challenges and structure of your business

   b. Understand the goals, strategies, and policies that your organization is trying to gain

   c. Demonstrate a strong sense of commitment to those outcomes into a reality

   d. Act as a neutral third party instead of a barrier to business development and growth

   e. Identify the Cybersecurity metrics that are most relevant and compelling to the other members of the C-Suite

The Quantitative Backup

As mentioned earlier in this chapter, I have been a technical writer for Cybersecurity for 13 years now. I have written a ton of stuff, and whenever people make claims to hypotheses they formulate, I always like to see some quantitative back to it. Such is the case with the last section. True, anybody can throw out into the ring what a CISO should do to improve their tenure rate and face less of a burnout rate. But the hypotheses given in the last section have been backed up by a true, scientific study.

Here are the findings:

1) "Top-tier CISOs are 266% more likely to be dramatically increasing their 2019 security budgets.
2) Top-tier CISOs are 93% more likely to measure and report vulnerabilities found and blocked.
3) Top-tier CISOs are 52% more likely to have purchased an end-to-end integrated security solution.
4) Top-tier CISOs are 45% more likely to have a security architecture with full centralized visibility and control.
5) Top-tier CISOs are 35% more likely to address risk proactively – from detection to remediation.
6) Top-tier CISOs are 27% more likely to measure risk and align their security program against risk tolerance.
7) Top-tier organizations are 26% more likely to measure productivity gains from their security solutions.
8) Top-tier CISOs are 25% more likely to have robust protection against known and unknown threats"."

(Source: 11)

Finally to conclude this chapter, a CISO must not only have a great technical background but must understand the business perspective of their job as well in order to communicate their visions and plans. This is nicely summed up by the following quote:

> The CISOs role is an ultimate support function for each and every part of the organization. He or she needs to have a strong business background as well.
>
> **(Source: 12)**

But in the end, having a balance of both worlds is hard, thus leading to the CISO quitting or getting terminated and wanting he or she to start their own business. But to start one, you first need to have a good business plan. This is the topic of Chapter 2.

Further Reading

1. https://corporatefinanceinstitute.com/resources/careers/jobs/what-is-a-ceo-chief-executive-officer/
2. https://corporatefinanceinstitute.com/resources/careers/jobs/what-does-a-cfo-do/
3. https://corporatefinanceinstitute.com/resources/careers/designations/chief-operating-officer-coo/
4. https://corporatefinanceinstitute.com/resources/careers/designations/c-suite/
5. https://corporatefinanceinstitute.com/resources/careers/designations/c-suite/
6. https://www.indeed.com/hire/c/info/role-of-cio
7. https://www.csoonline.com/article/3245170/why-do-cisos-change-jobs-so-frequently.html
8. https://www.itgovernance.co.uk/cyber-resilience
9. https://xgrcsoftware.com/what-is-vendor-compliance-management/
10. "The Evolution of the CISO", by Bitsight
11. The CISO and Cybersecurity: A Report on Current Priorities and Challenges" by Fortinet
12. Engel, Barack. *Why CISOs Fail.*, CRC Press, 2018.

Chapter 2

The Business Plan

In the previous chapter of this book, we carefully examined those factors that lead to CISO burnout and eventual termination or quitting. We also pointed out various facets that a CISO can use to lengthen their tenure at their place of employment, if that is what they choose to do. But just suppose you are that CISO who was recently terminated or you just simply quit because of burnout. What do you do next?

Well, this is much more of a subjective issue that you are going to have to reflect on more, obviously. Perhaps talking about it with family and close friends can help give you an answer. Or you could even work with a career counselor to help you decide what you want your next steps to be. Or maybe you have had thoughts of returning back into the CISO role, but at a different company.

But perhaps you have not explored another yet and that is to start your own business. Sure, this may sound like a daunting and insurmountable task, but truth be told, there are many ex-CISOs out there who still want to stay in Cybersecurity but, instead, want to take the plunge and start their own business. Given just how digital everything is today, getting the resources to formally start your new Cyber Consulting business is actually much easier now than it used to be.

DOI: 10.1201/9781003305309-2

For example, you can go off Google and pretty much find all of the resources you need in order to launch your new venture. Heck, you can even create your business entity online as well. But, even despite all of these advantages, it is important that you follow a process of steps in order to make sure that you have not left out any important steps.

In this regard, the first step is seeking the services of a good business attorney and/or accountant (and if you can get both, that would be even more ideal). You might be thinking now that investing in these professionals to help you out sounds like an expensive proposition. But truth be told, they are really not that bad. Most accountants and lawyers have even quit their own day jobs to start their own professional firm in this era known as the "Great Resignation", which has been catalyzed by the COVID-19 pandemic. They too are also entrepreneurs, and realize that you will have a budget.

So, how much am I talking about here? Well, from beginning to end, we are probably talking about $500 to $600 tops, and this is a flat fee. This means that all of their services are bundled, and you do not pay anymore unless you want more done. One of the exceptions to this is the filing fees at the state level. Also, try to find a lawyer and accountant who can work with you for the long haul. They can become your crucial allies, especially when it comes to business expansion, hiring new employees, and yes, filing those dreaded business tax returns every March 15th.

For my Cybersecurity Consulting practice, I have an attorney who I have worked with for 13 years, though my accountant keeps changing every now and then. Oh yea, here is another reason why you want to make use of one of these professionals, especially the attorney. When you file your formal business structure, you have to have what is known as a "Registered Agent". This must be a real person, with a permanent brick-and-mortar structure in the state in which you file.

Essentially, this person who you select becomes the point of contact to which papers will be served, in case you are named in a lawsuit. But there is yet another benefit here as well. Suppose you move out of the state of your business and decide to settle somewhere else. Rather than dissolving your existing legal entity, and starting from scratch all over again, you can still keep this same legal entity, because your Registered Agent still resides there with that business address. Just one less thing to worry about in case you are in this situation. And, from a tax perspective, in case you are ever audited by the Internal Revenue Service (IRS), your accountant can pretty much take care of things for you also, which even includes receiving correspondence on your behalf, so that you can stay focused on your business. So, you may be wondering at this point, what are these steps you need to take that will lead to the launch of your new Cybersecurity Consulting business?

This chapter will only provide the most important highlights. In the end, your lawyer and/or accountant will literally take your hand and guide you through every nuance and every nook and cranny that you need to go through in order to make sure that you are up to snuff with everything. So, here we go.

What Should I Focus My Business On?

As a CISO, your career has spanned a very long and broad horizon. You have probably picked up a lot of technical skills that your college degree did not train you for, and hopefully you have also picked up a lot of management skills that no MBA program can ever teach you. At least, this is the case with me, especially with the latter. What I am trying to get at here is that you now have a wide skillset that you can really use now to launch and propel your new business.

But rather than being the proverbial jack-of-all-trades, master of none, it is important to stay focused in this regard. Put it another way, the world of Cybersecurity is a huge one, with many different positions in it. You probably have gained a flavor of all of these different roles by being that CISO. But now you have to take stock of where your particular strengths and weaknesses are at. Once again, talking about this with a career counselor and even your family and close friends can be a big help to you.

But the important thing here is to literally take an honest look in the mirror at yourself. Be brutally honest to yourself as to what you know you can do well at and those things that you cannot do so well at. In this regard, I am also honest with myself. Yes, people have told me that I excel at tech writing, but I know that I could never be a programmer. I simply do not have the mindset for that. Also, I know that I could never be an RFP (Request For Proposal) writer either. I tried doing that and utterly despised it.

So, in your long or short tenure as a CISO, take a look at what you have enjoyed doing and not enjoyed doing. Then make a list of all of these. Once you have compiled this list, pay particular attention to your strengths. This is what you will be using partially, in order to help you decide what kind of Cyber-related products and services you want to offer.

Now we come to this point. What should you specifically offer? Once again, here you have to go back to that list. Look at those technical areas in which you have excelled. Then from there, pick those one or two things that you think you are very good at from the technical perspective. This could be anything from deploying tools and technologies to calculating Cyber Risk, establishing the proper set of controls to protect digital and physical assets, conducting audits to make sure that you have come into compliance with the data privacy laws such as those of the GDPR, CCPA, HIPAA, etc., doing Penetration Testing and Threat Hunting, conducting Cloud deployments and migrations, and coming into compliance with the nuances and confusions surrounding the Cybersecurity Maturity Model Certification (CMMC) for the Department of Defense, you name it.

But as you pick out what you are going to offer, the key thing to keep in mind is how you are going to differentiate yourself from the rest of the crowd. In this regard, it is very important to keep in mind that there are some 2,000+ Cybersecurity vendors alone here in the United States. So how are you going to differentiate yourself from them? The key here is to evaluate this from both the qualitative (in other words, the human aspect) and the technical aspects. With the former, here are two key areas that could help you based upon my experiences:

■ Stay focused exclusively on customer service. In other words, keep things to a level that your client and/or prospect can understand. The world of Cybersecurity is full of nonsensical techno jargon, and to be honest, people are getting sick of it. Your customers/prospects want to know in clear simple terms how they can benefit from your services and products, and how you plan to deliver them. Resist using these techno jargon terms as much as possible. And even after you have engaged, keep the conversations, dialogues, and most importantly, your relationship with your customers in this regard. This will yield far more results than dazzling them with the latest and greatest.

■ Try to focus on those untapped markets. Yes, you are in business to make money, and you want to make a profit to stay afloat, and hopefully much more than that. Unfortunately, in this regard, many of the Cyber vendors who I know of only focus on those industry verticals and segments that are large and which will give them a good profit margin. A typical example of this is the Fortune 500. But the bad news here is that since there are so many of these Cybersecurity vendors vying for this market, it is becoming too competitive. For example, if you do end up getting a large client, and they are not happy with your services, they simply ditch you and go with a competitor in a matter of minutes. Therefore, you want to find that market in which your customers will stick with you. In this regard, a great market is the small-to-medium-sized (SMB) business. True, they may not have large budgets and you probably won't make a lot of money off in the beginning, but as you build up and cultivate your relationships with them for the long term, they will stick with you, because they know and trust you and highly value your company name. The SMB market still remains a very much untapped one and will probably be so for the long term. But also keep this perspective in mind: Always think for the long term and never for the short term alone.

■ Just offer one or two products and/or services. As I just mentioned, there are tons of Cybersecurity vendors here in the United States. They all try to offer many services to customers and prospects. While the intention here is to be a one-stop Cyber shop for them, this can totally backfire in the end. And, I am speaking from experience on this one. A few years ago, I tried offering a bunch of other Cybersecurity services as well but was going nowhere with it, and that is until the day a few good friends knocked some sense into me: Just stick to what you do well, even if it is just doing one thing. And to me, that meant focusing exclusively on technical writing, along with podcasting. In this regard, try to take this same approach. In the beginning, you will most likely be a one-man band, so you can't spread yourself too thin. Also, in whatever vertical and industry you choose to serve, try to pick an area of Cybersecurity that no other vendor is offering. For example, if there are ten vendors offering all Penetration Testing services, then offer something close, but different, like just Threat Hunting. In other words, rather than wasting time and money to come up with an entirely new product or service, just build a better mousetrap. Chapter 3 of this book goes into one such area, which is Threat Research and Modeling. In my years in Cybersecurity, I have only known very few people that offer this service exclusively. That is why I picked this area for you to possible start in.

Ok, now that you have selected those markets you want to serve and have also finalized those one or two things you want to offer to prospects and customers; now is the time to pick the type of business entity that will serve you the best.

Choosing the Legal Business Entity

Now that you have decided what you want your new Cybersecurity Consulting business to focus on after taking stock of all your strengths and weaknesses; the next step now is to decide how you formally want to structure your business. You might be asking at this point what I mean by this? Well, you want to have your business have some sort of legal structure. This makes it not only easy from an accounting and tax standpoint but will also give the image to your customers and prospects that you are the so-called "real deal" and not some fly-by-night company.

In today's Cybersecurity world, customers want to know that you will be around for the long haul (at least in theory), and choosing that right setup will carry dividends for you in the end in this regard. So, what are the choices that you have? Here we go.

The Different Kinds of Entities

1) *The Sole Proprietorship*

This form is owned by one person who reports all business profits or losses on their individual tax return. Typically, this is done on Schedule C. Technically, this is the simplest and easiest business to set up. All you have to do is merely file very minimal paperwork with your local county government and you are off to go. But there is a huge risk in this: You have unlimited liability. This means that if you are named in a lawsuit, all of your assets are at risk, even your personal ones.

2) *Limited Liability Company*

This is also known as an "LLC" for short. Legally, it is a hybrid business structure that protects the personal assets of the owners (called members) just like how a corporation would, but allows for any profits or losses to flow straight down to your individual tax return. In other words, the LLC does not pay any taxes. If you have a profit, that is added to your Adjusted Gross Income (AGI), and any losses can be deducted from that as well.

3) *The C Corporation*

When you first incorporate, this is the legal formation that you have. The best thing about this is that your company assets and personal assets are all separate from one another. So, if you are named in a lawsuit, only your company assets are at risk, not your personal ones. Other advantages include:

a. The ability to issue multiple classes of stock;
b. Have an unlimited number of shareholders.
    But the disadvantages include the following:
a. Profit is taxed once on the business level;
c. Profits are also taxed on an individual basis when earnings are distributed to shareholders.

The above is also known as "Double Taxation", which can hit business owners hard, because you are taxed twice. But there is a way around this, known as the "S Corporation".

4) *The S Corporation*

An S Corporation because into being once you have filed the right forms with the IRS (which is form 2553). This is actually in many ways like an LLC, in that you have limited liability and all profits or losses flow directly down to your personal tax return. But there are some disadvantages to this as well, which are as follows:

a. Only one class of stock can be issued and you cannot have more than 100 shareholders;

b. A for-profit business cannot have ownership in an S Corporation (but an LLC can have this).

In the next subsection, we do a deep dive into the benefits and advantages of the LLC, C Corporation, and S Corporation.

The LLC

Here are the advantages:

1) *Limited Liability*

The members are also the owners of the LLC, and just like an S Corporation, they are not personally liable for the actions of the company. What this means is that your personal assets are fully protected from any creditors that are seeking to collect from the business. This protection stays in as long as you run your business like a business, which primarily means keeping business and personal financials separate.

2) *Pass-Through Taxation on Profits*

All profits and losses go directly to its members without being taxed by the IRS at the company level. Instead, members pay tax on the profits or any deductions on losses on their own federal income tax returns.

3) *Management Flexibility*

All documented members can manage an LLC, which allows all owners to have a stake in the business's day-to-day decision-making activities.

In many states, an LLC is member-managed by default unless explicitly stated otherwise in the Articles of Organization.

4) *Easy Startup and Upkeep*

The initial paperwork and filing fees for an LLC are relatively light when compared to that of the corporation. The only document that needs to get filed after you have created and started the LLC is the Annual Report, which gets filed once a year. On a personal note, I have known many Cyber business owners who started off as an S Corporation but later reverted to the LLC because of its requirement of lack of administrative maintenance.

Disadvantages

1) *The Loss of Limited Liability*

A judge, even at a whim, can rule that your LLC structure doesn't protect your personal assets. This is known as "piercing the corporate veil". This happens when you don't distinctly separate business transactions from personal transactions or comingle assets.

2) *The Repercussions of Member Turnover*

Generally speaking, if a member leaves the company, the LLC must be dissolved, no matter what. The other members can still do business, but they will have to start a brand-new LLC all over again.

The S Corporation

Here are the advantages

1) *Pass-Through Status*

Just like an LLC, if you structure your business as an S Corporation, you only pay taxes only on the money that you make from your business, and you can also take any losses as deductions as direct losses on income, which can actually lower your tax bill.

2) *Limited Liability*

The shareholders of an S Corporation are not personally liable for any actions of the company. This means that the owners' personal assets are protected as long as you run your business like a business.

Here are the disadvantages

1) *Restrictions on Shareholders*
   As mentioned, you can only have 100 shareholders. This can put a severe crimp on future growth. Keep in mind that the shareholders have to be individuals and not businesses. Thus raising investments can be much harder and take more time.
2) *Administrative Complexity*
   When compared to the LLC, the amount of paperwork and other administrative duties can be very tedious. For example, you have to file separate Sub S tax returns, hold annual meetings, record any new actions as minutes, etc. But these vary from state to state, and there is no set standard in this regard.

The C Corporation

Here are the advantages

1) *Unlimited Investors*
   You can have as many investors as are willing to purchase a part of your company. Those shareholders can be businesses or individuals and foreign or domestic. You can also offer different classes of stock, which makes it a very attractive option for Venture Capitalists and Angel Investors.
2) *Minimize Health-Care Costs*
   As an owner of a C Corporation, you can actually deduct your health-care insurance premiums from it, which means that it is a fully deductible amount on your corporate tax return.

Here are the disadvantages

1) *Double Taxation of Profits*
As mentioned before, double taxation is the main disadvantage here. For example, if it makes a profit, the IRS will tax it. Then, if you and other investors take a dividend, those proceeds are taxed again on your personal tax returns and theirs.
2) *Complexity*
Running a C Corporation in a legally compliant manner can be just as much or even more complex than running an S Corporation.

So, as you can see, choosing the right legal entity for your Cybersecurity Consulting business is not something to be taken lightly. There are various factors to be weighed, and that is why you should have a business attorney. Not only can they help you decide which is the right one for you, but they can also file the necessary paperwork with your Secretary of State's office. But truthfully speaking and as mentioned before, many owners of Cybersecurity businesses are now opting for the LLC – because of its flexibility and lesser administrative duties.

Getting the FEIN Number

Once you have selected and filed the paperwork for your legal structure, the next step in the process is to get your Federal Employment Identification Number, also known as the "FEIN" for short. This is like the Social Security number for your business, and this is what is used in all correspondence with the IRS and your state taxation office, as well as when it comes to filing both your federal and state business tax returns (assuming you have chosen either an LLC or an S Corporation or a C Corporation).

You obtain your FEIN number through the IRS website, or your attorney and/or accountant can do it for you as well by filing form SS-4.

Your Business's Website

Once you have the above pieces more or less situated, the next item you need to give very careful thought about is your website for your new Cybersecurity Consulting business. Now, I am not a web designer by any means, but I have dealt a lot with my own enough that I can offer some sage advice in this regard. The bottom line is that your website is going to be a reflection of you and how you plan to offer your services. There is really no right way or wrong way in creating and launching your website, but it's important to take some of these pointers I am about to offer into serious consideration.

After all, your website is going to be like your $24 \times 7 \times 365$ sales rep, so you need to keep it clean and simple. Here we go:

1) *Pick a Good Hosting Provider*

A simple Google search can reveal to you all of the top web hosting providers that are out there. Of course, they want your business, so they are going to offer you the cheapest price on everything you want to get because you will be a new customer. But be very careful of this. While this is very tempting, remember this old adage: You get what you pay for. Before you choose a hosting provider, make sure to closely examine the Google reviews. Of course, there will be negative comments, as you can't make everybody happy. But if the good reviews outweigh the bad ones, then they are worth considering. But one other key aspect that you need to keep in mind is the kind of support you will be getting. In this regard, IMHO, the two best hosting providers are Namecheap and GoDaddy. They provide $24 \times 7 \times$

365 technical support, but the problem with Namecheap is that they are only available by chat. But, whenever I have needed their services, they have been great. With GoDaddy, you have both phone and chat support. So, if I had to recommend to you which one to go with, it for sure would be one of these two. Namecheap is more limited in its hosting plans, but once again, they are a rock-solid hosting provider.

2) *Pick a Good Domain*

This can be a very tricky one to decide upon, as there are now a ton of domain extensions that you can pick from. You can use any of these new ones for your initial domain, but believe it or not, is still the ".com" that is favored the most, even after well over 20 years of being in service since the height of the Internet bubble. So take a scan of all of the domain extensions that you are interested in, and even call the hosting provider that you have signed up with for advice. In this regard, GoDaddy even has dedicated domain specialists that can help you out to a great extent. But, in the end, as far as possible, try to get a ".com" domain extension, as that will be of help in your SEO efforts. Now, what about the actual domain name itself? In the end, it is up to you to pick what you want, but the recommendation would be to use the name of your company, in some varying combinations. Speaking of which, the name that you pick for your company is going to be very important as well. But as far as possible, based upon my own experiences, try to stay away from using "Cyber" or "Information Security". These names are really beaten up and used quite a bit, so you want to use something that is refreshing and offers hope for the future. The name that you pick for your company is something that should not be taken lightly, and in fact, this is probably one of the hardest decisions that you will be making as you launch your business. My suggestion here would be to pick a few names that have both meaning and relevance to you and put that up to a vote with your family and close friends.

3) *Start Creating the Website*

Admittedly, this is one of the hardest parts to accomplish. The reason for this is that there are so many ways in which you can get this done. When you first sign up with a web hosting provider (like Namecheap or GoDaddy), more than likely you will be offered some sort of starter package in which you can build your website from various templates. I actually have gone this route for many of my one-page sites, but for the main website, my recommendation would be to hire a professional to do it. In this regard, I don't mean hiring your best friend to do it, but what I mean is finding a solid web design company that has been doing this for a long time. Make sure to ask for references from them and check them out. Now here is where most people will be hesitant: The price. Yes, going with a professional web design company is not going to be cheap, but there are ones out there who specialize in people just like yourself who are first starting out. There are two reasons for this: Your website is going to grow over time, and you want somebody for the long term who will help you do this. Second, keep in mind that while the initial costs may seem higher out of your budget, you can write this off as a direct expense when you file your business's first year's tax returns. Now, here is yet another key piece of advice: Keep the design of your website simple and easy to navigate through. Why do I say this? Cybersecurity companies are notorious for having huge and complex websites. They feel that they have to put everything up including the kitchen sink. Sure, you want to portray yourself as the expert, but this tactic is only going to backfire. Believe me, I have been a victim of this myself. If your site is too packed with stuff, any prospect will simply log off from it. In the end, all they want to really see is what you offer, what makes you different from the rest of the

2,000+ Cybersecurity vendors that are out there, and how to contact you. If they cannot get all of this within the first 5 minutes since initially going to your site, you will have lost a prospect. So, here is what the basic layout of the initial website should look like:

a. The Home Page
b. The About Us Page
c. The Our Services Page
d. The Contact Us Page

Yep, you got it. Just four basic pages, at least in the beginning. But as mentioned, it will grow from there. In the end, your website is just a lead-generation tool, in which they can contact you. Then you contact them back and get the ball rolling to cultivate that prospect into a client. Also, keep in mind that the design of the website is going to be very important. This is where the role of UI/UX will come into play. This is simply an acronym that stands for "User Interface/User Experience". Make sure that the web development company you hire is well versed in this. Keep the design of your website clean, and always avoid using flashy images or other gimmicky items. Not only will this slow down the load times of your website, but it can also be quite irritating to the prospect who is visiting it. From my own experiences, if I come across a website like this, I simply steer away from it by clicking on the "X" on the upper-right-hand side. One more piece of advice: Avoid having video come up as the first thing when a prospect loads up your website. This simply startles him or her and will be a huge turnoff. Also, make sure to see mockups of any web design before you go live with it.

4) *Content Creation*

As I mentioned earlier, Cybersecurity vendors are notorious for making their websites like Google. While having lots of information on your site can be a good thing, in the end, it can be a very negative thing. For example, it is quite easy for a prospect to get lost in all of this mess.

And if they cannot figure out what you do and offer for them, you have lost them permanently. So at least for the initial launch of your website, try to keep the content very easy to understand, and put up just enough so that people will know who you are and what you do. Remember, the ultimate goal is to make your website into a lead-generation tool and just a repository for free information. Now, here comes another very tricky area that your web development company is going to oversell you on: SEO and Google Rankings. I am not at all by any means an SEO expert, but the ultimate goal here is to put enough keywords in your initial website content so that you get ranked on the first page of Google whenever a prospect does a search. This is no doubt important, but by no means should you be obsessed by this and make this your first priority. Being ranked high in Google can take up to months, and once you get up there, you can be down in the rankings in just a short period of time. There is nothing permanent about this. So, be extremely careful if your web development company is overpumping this to you. Keep this as a long-term goal, and nothing more than that. I have seen Cybersecurity companies that were simply obsessed with being high in the Google Rankings and nothing else. You know what happened to them? They lost focus on what their primary bread and butter is and lost customers. Building great relationships comes down to one thing: Honesty and transparency. Not the Google Rankings. Now the next question that often comes up is how to write the content. In this regard, you want to be as nontechnical as possible, as you simply do not know who will be visiting your site. In this regard, it is best to have a copywriter do this for you, and your web development company should have somebody on staff who can help you do this. But of course, as you start putting up blogs and whitepapers on your site, these should be written by you, as you want prospects to see that you are a thought leader in your Cyber field.

5) *Social Media*

Using social media can be both a good thing and in today's times a very bad thing. Cybersecurity companies feel that they need to get their name out as much as possible; so they will try to be on every major social media platform possible. But this is not needed. IMHO, the two that you should use primarily are Twitter and Linked In. The former is great in blasting about company news, any new products or services that you will be offering, and if you will be having a sponsor table at an upcoming trade show. But it is the latter that works best for the Cybersecurity Industry. It is great for the following reasons:

a. The venue is for professional views only, and not the nonsense that you see on Facebook.

b. You can post articles.

c. You can create a separate company page for your Cybersecurity Consulting business.

d. You can even create a forum or forums in which you can invite other members to join and share other Cyber thoughts and views.

e. You can quickly and easily network with other colleagues in the Cybersecurity Industry.

You also should never have more than two social media accounts linked to your website. The primary reason for this is that the Cyberattacker of today is actually scraping through social media accounts of unsuspecting victims so that they can build up a profile of them over time. The intention here is to eventually find any weak spots that are revealed in what is posted and use that to penetrate their way into the victim. And of course, the more social media profiles advertised, this simply increases your vulnerability surface.

6) *An Online Store*

Depending upon which area of Cybersecurity your business is going to focus on, you may even want to have an online store from which customers can buy your products and services directly. This should only be viewed as an add-on, and you probably will not need one in the very early stages of your Cybersecurity Consultancy. Your web hosting provider should have an E-Commerce package that you can use to create an online store in a short period of time, that, at the same time, also makes sure that all confidential data and information remain safe.

Establishing Payment Terms and Hiring Employees

Setting Up Payment Terms

As you launch your new Cybersecurity Consulting business, one of the next things before you start actually marketing your products and services is deciding upon how you will get paid for your services rendered. In the world of Cybersecurity, the one common mantra is that prospects and/or new clients always want something free first. In my world of Cyber tech writing, I have experienced this all over. For example, people always want a free sample. I used to do that but, in the end, got burned. So, I have stopped doing that, and if a prospect wants a free sample, they can visit a dedicated microsite for that.

But for the CISO, your prospects will obviously want something else. They may want a free assessment first in order to get a flavor of what you can offer, or they may want some sort of free audit to get a quick checkup on their security controls. This is all fine, and most Cybersecurity vendors actually do this. But as mentioned, there has to be a line drawn as to how much you can give for free. After all, you have a business, and your ultimate goal is to make money.

So, depending upon what you have to offer, my recommendation would be to stop at just one free thing. After that, the new client has to pay. If there is pushback on this, then simply say you can't give away everything for free. So in this regard, you need to decide what your payment terms will be. In the world of Cybersecurity, most vendors usually start off with at least two different kinds of contracts, which are as follows:

- The Master Services Agreement: This stipulates the overall relationship that you will have with your new client (in a very broad sense).
- The Statement of Work: This spells out the work to be done, the time frame for delivery, how much your Service Fee(s) will be, the conditions for any additional charges, and the terms of payment.

True, there are many contractual templates online that you can use to create these documents. But it is always best to have your attorney do these for you. It is important to note that this will not be included in the flat incorporation fees, and your attorney will charge you separately for this. So ask how much it will first cost to draw up these contracts, and then set the money aside for getting these documents done.

Probably the best way to get started in terms of payment is to require half of the Service Fee upfront and the other half payable after the services have been rendered and completed. But of course, as time goes on, and if you have developed a rock-solid relationship with your clients, then you can modify this accordingly and maybe even throw in a discount or so. But initially, it is important that you stick to your payment terms with any new client.

Now, the next thing to consider is how you will receive your Services Fee. There are numerous ways that you can do this, and they are as follows:

- ACH
- Wire Transfer
- Check
- PayPal
- Credit Card

It's up to you the way in which you want to get paid. As for my Cyber business, I usually just use PayPal. It's easy to send out the invoices, and you receive the money into your account usually within one business day. But it is also important to ask your client what payment method works for them. For example, I have had some clients who do not use PayPal but use ACH, etc. So, you have to be flexible in that regard.

It is also important in the Master Services Agreement (MSA) that your attorney prepares for you the terms for collection and any penalties for any late payments.

Hiring New Employees

When you first open your doors, probably one of the next thoughts that will come to your mind is hiring employees. While this is a good sign that you are growing and expanding, lots of caution is needed here. Hiring employees is an entirely different ball game and one that you need to work with your accountant on very closely. For example, you have to be very careful about paying payroll taxes on time; if not, both the IRS and your state taxation office can come down on you hard.

So, my advice is at least in the beginning stages, to try to do all of the work as you can on your own. Once you have established enough revenue to hire some employees, then have that talk with your accountant. I have been working solo for the last 13 years, and while I have thought of bringing somebody else on board, I have so far resisted for these very reasons. Remember you can always hire employees as contractors or as direct hires, and each has both its advantages and disadvantages. But all of this is out of the scope of this book; so that is why your accountant and possibly even your attorney can be your best resources to turn to in this regard.

Another question that is going to pop up is business insurance and what kind to get. There are numerous and these include the following:

- General liability insurance
- Commercial property insurance
- Business income insurance
- Workers' compensation insurance
- Professional liability insurance
- Product liability insurance
- Employment practices liability insurance
- Errors and omissions insurance
- Cyber liability insurance
- Business identity insurance
- Commercial auto insurance
- Commercial fleet insurance
- Commercial umbrella insurance
- Key person insurance

While it is out of the scope of this book as well to tell you what you need, you always reach out to your existing insurance provider (such as the one that does your automobile insurance) for further advice. More than likely they will have what you need, if not, they can steer you in the right direction.

Do I Need a Brick-and-Mortar Presence?

Before the COVID-19 pandemic hit, most businesses had a traditional storefront. But with now everything being virtual and remote, many businesses have now opted to use what is known as "Virtual Offices". This is where you can rent office space for very cheap when and how you need it. But by being in Cybersecurity, everything is now done in the Cloud; so the chances of you needing a traditional brick-and-mortar presence really should not be there.

You should only consider getting one if you have grown to the point where you have multiple office locations and have many employees who need access to shared resources on the premises. For that matter, at the beginning and intermediate stages of your Cybersecurity Consultancy, try to make use of the Virtual Office option first.

The Financial Components of the Business Plan

While this chapter so far has reviewed some of the major components that should be included in your overall business plan, don't forget there is yet another key piece that needs to be in there as well. This is the financial aspect. After all, except for your customers, this can be considered to be the heart of your business. Without a good beat at it, it will be hard for your business to weather any storm that it might face down the road.

Now, of course, each business plan will vary in how it includes the financial components, but all of them share two common denominators, and they are as follows:

- The Profit and Loss Statement
- The Cash Flow Statement

We examine both of these in greater detail in the next two subsections.

The Profit and Loss Statement

The Profit and Loss Statement is simple by nature: You are merely forecasting your profit or loss for the future. The time horizon that you put on this is entirely up to you and the specific nature of your business. But at the very least, you should be projecting your profit or loss at least one month out. The Profit and Loss Statement consists of these three general categories:

- Sales Revenue: This is all of the money that your Cybersecurity Consulting business takes in, from all of the products and services that you sell.
- The Cost of Sales: This is the cost that is associated with selling your product or service. Very often, this is also referred to as the "Variable Costs".

■ The Fixed Costs: This can also be referred to as the "Overhead Costs", and no matter what, you must pay them on a regular basis, no matter how much you sell or not. As its name implies, these expenses are fixed in nature and do not change over time, unless you change your business processes.

The Fixed Expenses can be specifically broken down into the following subcategories:

1) *The Rent*

This is the monthly payment for your office space, whether it is a brick-and-mortar- or a Virtual Office-based one.

2) *The Wages and Payroll Taxes*

This is how much you pay your employees (whether it is on a biweekly/semiannual/or monthly basis) and the taxes that go with it (this includes Social Security, Medicare, Unemployment Benefits, etc.).

3) *The Marketing and Advertising*

These are all of the expenses that are tied with bringing your Cybersecurity Consultancy in front of the eyes of prospects, and even existing customers. This can run the gamut from hosting at a trade show to the costs associated with hosting your website, to even doing Email blasts (this would be the cost of your CRM System).

4) *The Accounting and Legal Expenses*

As its name implies, these are all the costs associated with your accountant and attorney who do the work for you. Your legal expenses will vary depending upon your specific needs, but most accounting expenses arise from business tax preparation and filing to all costs associated with your employee payroll.

5) *The Interest Expense*

This is the cost that is associated with any loans you have to pay back, whether it is from an investor or other financial institution.

6) *The Depreciation Expense*

This is the amount that you can deduct from your gross revenue if you make use of equipment or other related items, as it wears down over time.

7) *The Other Expenses*

These are the other expenses that you accrue into your business which need to be included in the Profit and Loss Statement but don't fall in the abovementioned categories.

The above categories are represented in the below matrix:

Total Sales Revenue
Cost of Sales
Gross Profit (Total Sales Revenue – Cost of Sales)
Fixed Expenses
Rent
Wages/Payroll Taxes
Marketing and Advertising
Business Insurance
Accounting and Legal
Interest
Depreciation
Utilities
Phone/Internet
Supplies
Other Expenses
Total Profit or Loss (Gross Profit – Total Fixed Expenses)

The Cash Flow Statement

The Cash Flow Statement merely represents the cash that you have coming in and going out of your business. It can be represented as follows:

Cash Coming In > Cash Going Out = A Positive Cash Flow
Cash Going Out > Cash Coming In = A Negative Cash Flow

The Cash Flow Statement consists of the following categories:

1) *The Profit or Loss*
    This value will come directly from your Profit and Loss Statement, as reviewed in the last subsection.
2) *The Credit Sales*
    This occurs when you sell any products to a customer but on a credit line that you have offered to them. This is also known as "Accounts Receivable".
3) *The Credit Collections*
    This value reflects how much your revenue will increase once you paid for a product that was sold via a credit line.
4) *The Credit Purchases*
This is when you purchase raw materials from a supplier, and they provide you with a line of credit from which you can purchase these items. Payment is usually due within 30 days after the raw materials have been purchased on credit. This category is also referred to as "Accounts Payable".
5) *The Payments for Credit Purchases*
    This is when you actually make payment for the raw materials you bought on credit from your supplier.
6) *The Withholding Tax*
    As it relates to your payroll, this is the portion that you pay for any taxes that is associated with Social Security and Medicare.
7) *The Withholding Tax Payments*
    This occurs when you pay the Withholding Taxes on a quarterly basis rather than the normal monthly basis.
8) *The Depreciation*
    This value is taken from the Profit and Loss Statement.

9) *The Loan Principal Payments*

This is the interest amount that you pay on any loans that you have incurred and is also taken directly from the Profit and Loss Statement.

10) *The Extra Purchases*

This is the value that reflects any credit or cash purchases you have made that do not fit in any of the categories as described in this subsection or the Profit and Loss Statement.

The above categories are represented in the below matrix:

Profit or Loss
Credit Sales (This is a negative value, so "−")
Credit Collections (This is a positive value, so "+")
Credit Purchases (This is a positive value, so "+")
Payments for Credit Purchases (This is a negative value, so "−")
Withholding Taxes (This is a positive value, so "+", assuming you pay quarterly)
Withholding Tax Payments (This is a negative value, so "−", assuming you pay quarterly)
Depreciation (This is a positive value, so "+")
Loan Principal Payments (This is a negative value, so "−")
Extra Purchases (This is a negative value, so "−")
Cumulative Net Cash (This is the final result when adding and subtracting the above values)

The Break-Even Point

Along with these statements just described, another key metric you need to compute is what is known as your "Break-Even Point". This is the point at which you make no actual profit or loss, and at some time after this has been achieved, it is expected that you will be on the way to making a profit. This is computed by the following formula:

Fixed Costs/Average Gross Profit=The Break-Even Sales Point

Further Reading

https://www.nerdwallet.com/article/small-business/how-to-start-a -business
McKeever, Michael P.. *How To Write A Business Plan*, NOLO, 2018.

Chapter 3

Launching the Threat-Hunting Business

As a former CISO, whether burned out or terminated, when you launch your new Cybersecurity Consultancy, there is a lot that you can offer, because you have a wide breadth and knowledge of experiences. But you want to be focused, so in this regard, one area in which you may want to first start off with is that of Threat Hunting. As mentioned, pretty much all Cybersecurity vendors offer the same thing. Your goal is to simply build a better mousetrap. So, focusing on Threat Hunting is one way to do it. This is what this chapter is all about. First, we start off with what it is all about.

Introduction

There is very often a fallacy in the world of Cybersecurity that simply implementing various types and kinds of Security Technologies towards the lines of defenses of a business or a corporation will mean greater levels of protection.

While in theory, this may be true, but reality often dictates the opposite of this. For example, by simply deploying various

DOI: 10.1201/9781003305309-3

Security tools, you are actually increasing the attack surface for the Cyberattacker.

For example, a CIO or a CISO may think that deploying ten firewalls is better than just having one in place. But with this thinking, they have given the Cyberattacker nine more avenues in which to attack the vulnerabilities and weaknesses of the IT Infrastructure.

Instead, it is far better to spend the critical financial resources for perhaps just two firewalls, *but making sure that they are strategically placed they are needed the most and will have the most effect.*

This kind of mindset of determining where Security Assets need to be placed is actually a very proactive one. The primary reason for this is that the CIO/CSIO and their IT Security staff are actually taking the time to discover what areas are most at risk in their organization, and what tools will be most effective and where, rather than spending money in a haphazard fashion.

In fact, this proactive way of thinking needs to be extended to the world of Threat Hunting as well. With this, the IT Security staff are using various kinds of methodologies and tools in order to scope out and mitigate the risks of any Cyber threats that are lurking from within their IT Infrastructure.

But being successful at doing this on a daily basis requires that the CIO/CISO and their IT Security staff have to go above and beyond the proverbial "extra mile". How this can be achieved is reviewed in this article.

A Formal Definition of Proactive Threat Hunting

A formal definition of proactive-based Threat Hunting is as follows:

> [It] is the process of proactively searching through networks or datasets to detect and respond to

advanced cyberthreats that evade traditional rule- or signature-based security controls. Threat hunting combines the use of threat intelligence, analytics, and automated security tools with human intelligence, experience and skills.

(Source: 1)

In other words, there are two subcomponents of this definition:

1) Being proactive in any type of Threat Hunting exercise means that the CIO/CISO has to break away from the conventional ways of thinking, and have the ability to "think out of the box". For instance, what works in one situation more than likely will not work in another, because the Cyber Threat Landscape is changing on a very dynamic basis.
2) Being proactive simply doesn't involve the use of the latest and most sophisticated of Threat Hunting tools. Rather, it takes not only that but also the use of reliable information and data as well as deep motivational levels, experience, and technical know-how from the IT Security staff.

Despite the importance of Threat Hunting in Cybersecurity today, not too many businesses and corporations are implementing it, which is pointed out by these stats in a recent survey in which 306 organizations were polled:

▪ Only 27% of the respondents actually had a well-defined Threat Hunting methodology and were actually utilizing it;
▪ Only 45% of the respondents had a formal plan in place in order to launch and execute a specific Threat Hunting exercise.

(Source: 2)

Other stats:

- 88% of businesses feel that their existing Threat Hunting approaches need to be greatly improved;
- 56% of organizations feel that conducting a Threat Hunting exercise with their own resources (or "in-house") takes too long and consumes resources from carrying out other IT Security-related duties;
- 53% of organizations feel that their Threat Hunting methodologies and activities are actually "tipping off" Cyberattackers.

(Source: 3)

Why are businesses and corporations not taking a proactive approach to Threat Hunting? The following reasons are cited:

1) The use of different tools can make Threat Hunting a very time-consuming proposition;
2) The collection of information and data can be a very labor-intensive process that requires third-party involvement and verification;
3) There is not enough time to conduct proactive-based Threat Hunting exercises because the IT Security staff has to respond to so many false alarms that are sounded off on a daily basis;
4) Because of the enormous time constraints that are involved, only about 1% of all Security Alerts are actually probed into and further examined;
5) Threat Hunting can be a huge financial drain;
6) Threat Hunting requires a very special kind of mindset – recruiting candidates for this specific talent can be very difficult.

(Source: 4)

Despite these abovementioned obstacles, proactive Threat Hunting is still a much-needed function for every business and corporation and is a process that can be achieved.

The Process of Proactive Threat Hunting and Its Components

Proactive Threat Hunting differs greatly from businesses to corporations, as to what needs to be specifically tracked down and mitigated depends largely upon their Security environment as well as their specific requirements. But in general terms, there are four major Proactive Threat Hunting categories, which are as follows:

1) *The Hypothesis-Driven Investigation*
   This is where it is discovered that a brand-new threat vector is imminent, based upon a rather significant information and data that is collected from the various Intelligence Feeds. Based upon this, the Threat Hunting team will then probe deeper into the network logs and attempt to find any hidden anomalies or trends that could be foretelling of a Cyberattack.
2) *The Indicators of Compromise (IOC) Investigation*
   This is when the Threat Hunting team does a "deep dive investigation" into the IT Infrastructure to determine where the malicious activity is specifically taking place, based upon the alerts and the warnings that they have received.
3) *The Analytics-Driven Investigation*
   This is where the Threat Hunting teams conduct targeted exercises based upon the information and the data that are collected from Machine Learning (ML), and Artificial Intelligence (AI) tools.

4) *The TTP Investigation*

TTP stands for Tactics, Techniques, and Procedures Threat hunting. This kind of Threat Hunting reveals the mannerisms in which a Cyberattacker operates. It is important to keep in mind that the Cyberattacker will not use the same toolset when launching another attack; rather, they will typically utilize the same operational techniques.

The general process for launching and executing a proactive Threat Hunting campaign is broken down into three distinct phases, which are as follows:

1) A specific alarm or trigger is set off, which guides the Threat Hunting team into the specific direction that they need to conduct their investigations into. More than likely, this will be an area in the IT Infrastructure or in the area of the Network Topology that has been deployed.
2) In the Investigative Phase, the Threat Hunting team will use sophisticated, analytical tools (an example of this is the use of Endpoint Detection and Response) in order to take that deep dive to pinpoint the source of the malicious activity. This activity will keep continuing until the source has been deemed to be non-malicious in nature, or a complete understanding of it has been developed.
3) In the Resolution Phase, the Threat Hunting team will then pass on what they have discovered to the Incident Response team so that they can mitigate the source of the malicious activity, as well as to conduct the appropriate response activities that are required.

In order to mount a successful and proactive Threat Hunting exercise, the following components are a must:

1) *Reliable Datasets*

They must be very granular in nature, and provide a complete and comprehensive picture of what the state of the network endpoints looks like, as most organizations tend to focus on the activities that take place in between the networks.

2) *Advanced Analytics*

The usage of these kinds of tools is required so that the various pieces of intelligence that are collected can be correlated with any Cyber threats that are coming from the external environment or any kinds of malicious behavior that might be exhibited.

3) *The Right Levels of Human Expertise and Talents*

This element is just as crucial or perhaps even more because proactive Threat Hunting is highly dependent upon both human interaction and collaborative teamwork.

Finally, based upon another survey:

■ 74% of businesses and corporations that have adopted a proactive Threat Hunting mindset have actually decreased their attack surface by at least 74% (which was discussed in the first section of this chapter).
■ 59% of organizations have actually increased the speed and timing it takes to respond to a Security Breach.

(Source: 3)

Hiring Your Threat Hunting Team

But keep in mind that Threat Hunting is something that you do not want to go alone with. You need to hire a good team, whether they are direct hires or just W2 or 1099 Contractors (keep in mind about hiring employees in Chapter 2, as it was reviewed). So here are some questions that you should ask the potential Threat Hunting candidates, in order to vet out the best ones.

Level 1 Questions

Question 1

Why do you want to become a Threat Intelligence Hunter? Is it the money that is making you attracted to this position?

Obviously, many Cybersecurity professionals apply for positions once they see the high salary levels that they can command for a particular role. But remember, the recruiter is wanting to understand your motive here as to why you are applying for this particular position. They want to see that you are attracted to this position not just from the standpoint of money. If this is the case, that is a huge red flag to them, as they know you will not stay for a long time. They want to know for sure that you will be around for quite some time, and will be a dedicated employee. The reason for this is that they will be also *making a substantial investment in you,* in order to bring you up to speed on the Security requirements of the organization.

Probably the best way to answer this question is to angle the answer as to how the company can benefit from your skillset. Tell them that you have a "burning" desire to help others and your company to fend off Cyberattacks, but above all, you also want to help protect their brand in the eyes of their customers.

Question 2

What makes your skill set different from the other candidates that we have looked at?

In this kind of question, the recruiter wants to see your confidence shine through, as there will be many other candidates applying for the same position as well. In other words, they want to see that one differentiating thing that separates you from the rest of the crowd. Yes, everybody will have certs, work experience, and some sort of educational degree, but you need to look into yourself as to what makes you different.

Question 3

What are the needed skills in order to be a successful Threat Intelligence Hunter?

It is important to keep in mind that becoming a successful Threat Intelligence Hunter in many ways is different than other Cybersecurity positions. For example, not only do you need a relatively strong quantitative background but you need to have exceptional qualitative skills. This is what the recruiter is trying to determine if you have this by asking this particular question. For instance, not only must you have a very keen eye in order to find unseen trends in the information and data that you collect but you must be able to break that down to a level that your client can understand as well. Also, you must have the ability and patience to work long hours, but most importantly, you must have that all-important investigative mind in order to thoroughly complete a Threat Hunting exercise.

Question 4

How do you deal with a difficult client? How do you address their needs?

By the tone of this particular question, this is obviously a psychological-based question. In this question, the recruiter is trying to determine your communications style. Remember, as mentioned before, not only will you be working with a dedicated team but you will also be interfacing directly with the client. Many times, the client can be difficult to work with. For example, there may be risks out there in their organization that you want to further investigate. But the client may be demanding and want something else checked out. Perhaps the best way to answer this question is that you should offer the client different options as to what should be investigated, and what you think is important. But remember in the end, it is the client that has the final say so in what will be examined, as they will be signing the documents that lay out the Statement and Scope of Work. If you step out of these bounds without prior client approval, you put not only yourself but the business or corporation that you work for at grave risk for a major lawsuit.

Question 5

What Is Threat Hunting?

You can be guaranteed that this will be one of the first questions that will be asked of you. The recruiter is not just looking for a memorized, textbook answer; rather they are examining to see if you can give a simple explanation if asked, especially by your client. A possible answer is:

> Threat hunting is the process of seeking out adversaries before they can successfully execute an attack.

(Source: 4)

This answer, while very broad in nature and scope, is succinct and to the point. You basically want to phrase it in such a way that the bottom line (or the primary goal of it) is to literally "hunt down" those Cyber threats that appear to be imminent on the horizon and mitigate them before they execute their malicious payload and cause widespread damage to the IT Infrastructure.

Question 6

What is the difference between Threat Hunting and other Prevention and Detection-based methods?

In this kind of question, the recruiter wants to make sure that you have a good understanding of how Threat Hunting is different from other methodologies, and why it is so important to their particular organization. A good answer here would be to state that Threat Hunting is very much a proactive Security Methodology that makes use of sophisticated analytical tools (such as those of Artificial Intelligence and Machine Learning). The Threat Hunting process first starts with formulating a specific hypothesis, in which the catalyst for this was some kind of alert, assessment, or even the results of a Penetration Test. This hypothesis will then be tested by using the abovementioned tools to search for this potential Cyber threat that has not been formally detected yet.

Question 7

What is the primary difference between Threat Hunting and Threat Detection?

Although these two sound very similar among one another, they are actually very different. The answer here is Threat Hunting is geared towards the *potential determination* of Cyber-related threats at their earliest stages possible. With Threat Detection, *an actual Cyber threat has been found*, and all efforts are dedicated in order to mitigate it.

Question 8

What are some of the benefits of Threat Hunting?

Obviously, the main benefit of Threat Hunting is that you are taking a proactive stance on the Cybersecurity Landscape to see what potential threats are possible lurking from within your IT Infrastructure. But it is important to keep in mind that the recruiter is trying to test if your understanding of Threat Hunting goes much deeper than just the obvious. In order to prove your level of expertise, you could mention some statistics such as the following:

According to a recent SANS survey:

- Clients reduced their attack surface by at least 75%.
- 59% of respondents felt that Threat Hunting greatly improved their Incident Response timing.

- 52% of respondents found Cyber threats via Threat Hunting; otherwise, they would not have been detected by other means.

(Source: 5)

Question 9

What are some of the drawbacks of Threat Hunting?

Of course, Threat Hunting has its flip side as well. This is very important in communicating to the client, as they should *not be given the impression* that each and every potential will be detected. The recruiter who is interviewing you wants to make sure that you fully understand this. A good answer here would be to state that (once again, citing a few stats will show your expertise):

- From the same survey as mentioned previously, 88% of the clients polled felt that their Threat Hunting processes needed some serious improvement.
- 53% of the respondents felt that their Threat Hunting processes were too transparent to the outside world.
- 56% of the respondents felt that the Threat Hunting process takes too long, and is still very cumbersome.

Question 10

What makes your cert different than the others that are other there?

In the world of IT Certification today, there are tons of certs that one can get. While you should strive to get a cert that is related to the Cybersecurity career you choose to aspire to, in the end, you can really choose to get any cert that you want to get. In the field of Threat Hunting, there is a premier cert that is known as the "Certified Cyber Threat Hunting Professional (CCTHP)". If you have this cert, or are at least planning to get it, you need to specifically bring this out in your interview. For example, you need to tell the recruiter that in the field of Threat Hunting, this is the premier cert to have. For example, it demonstrates that you have top-level and expertise knowledge in Threat Hunting, as it covers five, very specific domains that include the following:

- The goals/objectives of Threat Hunting
- The methodologies and techniques that are specifically utilized
- How to hunt for Network-based Cyber threats
- How to hunt for Host-based Cyber threats
- The tools and technologies that are used in Threat Hunting exercises

Level 2 Questions

Question 1

What is the primary difference between Threat Hunting and Penetration Testing?

Very often, these two types of Security Methodologies are used together; but in reality, they are totally different. Although the ultimate goal or outcome of both of these is to unearth any unknown Cyber-based threats or risks, Penetration Testing involves trying to break through an organization's lines of defenses. You are trying to see how far you can go in, without being detected. In other words, with Penetration Testing, you are taking an outside-in approach. But with Threat Hunting, this is much more of an inside – out to approach. For example, you are taking the assumption (or more specifically the hypothesis), that an adversary could already be lurking from within your IT Infrastructure; thus, you are taking steps to ascertain that. If your hypothesis is indeed confirmed, you then will try various attempts to mitigate them, so that they can penetrate from the outside environment ever again.

Question 2

Is Threat Hunting simply just devoted to finding internal Cyber threats, or does it involve more than just that?

In this kind of question, the recruiter is trying to determine (generally speaking) the depth of your Threat Hunting knowledge. The answer to this is yes, you are trying to find them, but there is much more involved than that. For example, with the information and data that you have collected, part of your other job responsibilities is to sift through it and determine any unseen trends with the analytical tools that you have on hand. With this, you should also be able to ultimately create various models of the future Cyber Threat Landscape, which will be indicative of what potential Cyberattacks could be like down the road for your organization.

Question 3

What happens if I don't find anything in the Threat Hunting Exercise that I have just engaged in?

Yes, it is theoretically possible to not find anything at all and to prove the hypothesis was false. Was this a complete waste of time then? No, not at all. There is a very good chance that you discover other kinds of Security Vulnerabilities which you thought never existed before. For instance, suppose that your Threat Hunt reveals something else, such as that there is an abnormally larger amount of bandwidth that is being used by other employees of the company. You report this to your CIO or CISO, and they want more analysis done. A further investigation reveals that many of them are using the FTP Protocol to back up their work-related files. This would obviously be a complete violation of your Security Policies, and as a result, you have discovered that "Shadow IT" is clearly evident in your company (this is when employees use non-authorized IT tools to conduct work-related duties).

Question 4

What is the ATT&CK Framework?

This is an expansive Threat Hunting Methodology that stands for "Adversarial Tactics, Techniques, and Common Knowledge". It was developed by the Mitre Corporation and has been around for quite some time. The basic premise of AAT&CK is to further break down Cyber threats into a multipurpose classification scheme, so that you can compare the information and data that is available here to what is actually transpiring with regards to threats and vulnerabilities in the Cyber environment of your organization. This is actually more of a knowledge base, and much more detailed information on it can be seen here, at this link.

Question 5

Should I just pick any random area of the ATT&CK Framework to start my Threat Hunting exercise?

While it is very important for the Threat Intelligence Hunter to have an overall open mindset, they should not just randomly pick something off of it and start looking around. Rather, you need to first analyze the log files (as well as the respective warnings and alerts) to see what trouble points exist. You also need to make sure that you have the right access permissions and privileges for those resources in which you need to conduct your Threat Hunt. For example, don't search for Account Manipulation adversaries if the access permissions and tools are not in place first. In other words, it is first very important to determine what you want to specifically achieve from your Threat Hunt. This is best accomplished by first formulating your hypothesis, as described earlier. It is important to keep in mind as well that a Threat Hunting exercise should be viewed as a scientific experiment: You are collecting information/data in order to prove or disprove your hypothesis. Also, be resourceful and use the other Security Technologies that you have on hand to further substantiate your hypothesis.

Question 6

Where does one draw the line between Threat Hunting and Incident Response?

Like Penetration Testing, there can be confusion between these two. Thus, it is important to keep in mind the literal meaning of these two terms. For instance, Threat Intelligence Hunters "hunt" for the adversaries that could be potentially lurking from within the IT Infrastructure, and to confirm their existence. The Incident Responders do just exactly that: They respond to Cyber threats once they have been alerted to that fact, and use the resources that they have at their disposal to mitigate them. Usually, it is the Incident Response Team that the Threat Hunting Team turns to first. The Threat Hunting Team should not be called upon to specifically mitigate a Cyber threat; rather, they should have the capabilities to work closely with the Incident Response to share their expertise in order to contain it.

Question 7

Should I move from left to right when using the ATT&CK Framework when executing my exercise?

Really, in the end, there is no specific order in which to move in ATT&CK. In other words, don't feel that you have to address each and every Cyber-related issue in the Framework, and above all, don't feel overwhelmed by it. Use the ATT&FM as a support anchor for your hypothesis, and start from there. If you don't have a hypothesis at first, then start your Threat Hunting exercise where you feel that your high-risk and first impact areas are in your IT Infrastructure, then work from a top-down approach from there. While speed is important in Threat Hunting, addressing issues in an incremental and accurate fashion is equally important. But if you feel that you must take a macro level when first assessing the Cyber threat environment, give serious consideration to using the methodology known as the "Mandiant Cyber Attack Lifecycle". More detailed information on this can be seen here.

Question 8

As we know, one of the ways a Cyberattacker can launch their specific threat vectors is through Privileged Escalation. What should a Threat Intelligence Hunter look for specifically in these instances?

There are different kinds of variables to look out for, but most importantly, a Threat Intelligence Hunter should first look into any known gaps or weaknesses that currently exist within the IT Infrastructure of an organization. In this instance, making use of an EDR solution (which can be viewed as a subset of Threat Hunting) would prove to be the most beneficial technique to be used. A Threat Intelligence Hunter should pay a lot of importance to what is known as "File Integrity Monitoring" (or FIM for short) on those IT Systems (for instance, servers) where the integrity of files should not be changing. If there are any suspicious changes to the files, a history of employee logins must be examined for any types of anomalous behaviors. Also, you should also check any systems that have been misconfigured, as this is another backdoor for the Cyberattacker to penetrate through.

Question 9

Should a Threat Intelligence Hunter just conduct their exercise in just one part of an Infrastructure, or should they be examining multiple areas?

Yes, by all means, a Threat Intelligence Hunter and the team should be examining different areas. Just because you have formulated a specific hypothesis, it doesn't mean that you should look in just one area. Rather, in order to get a comprehensive view of your IT Infrastructure, the Threat Intelligence Hunter needs to examine other areas, which for example include the normal, everyday IT Systems, the Virtual Machines, your Servers, and even your Production Environment, but make that in these instances, that you have the appropriate backups in place.

Question 10

What is the value of Threat Hunting if a business or corporation already has automated tools in place?

A popular, automated tool is known as "Cb Response". It helps to keep an eye on any intrusions into an organization 24 × 7 × 365. But keep in mind that systems like these can only provide information and data that is fed into it from the various intelligence feeds that you are currently making use of. But ultimately, it takes human intervention and a keen eye to further investigate the alerts and warnings that these systems provide. It is only through this process can one truly determine if a Cyber threat is imminent, or there is actually a threat actor that is lurking in your system.

Question 11

What are the two primary types of Threat Hunting Exercises?

There are two types as follows:

The On-Demand Investigation Mode
In this mode, Threat Hunting is used by IT Security teams to quickly investigate any suspicious or anomalous activities after they have been detected. Once the incident has been specifically identified, it is then passed to the

Security Operations Team for deeper investigation and recommendations for containment and recovery.

Continuous Monitoring or Testing Mode

In this model, the Security Operations team is continuously monitoring and/or testing their security posture by conducting various Penetration Testing exercises in order to proactively identify and investigate any suspicious events.

This newer type of approach may be initiated by the business entity itself, or it can be outsourced to a Managed Security Service provider.

Level 3 Questions

Question 1

Can you describe the five parts of the Threat Hunting Maturity Model?

Yes, there are five steps that are involved, and they are as follows:

- HMO-Initial

  At this stage, the organization is 100% dependent upon the use of automated tools, such as SIEMs and other AntiMalware/Spyware software packages in order to provide a warning and alert system.
- HM1-Minimal

  The organization is still heavily dependent upon the use of automated threat tools (as described above), but the IT staff is at least doing a minimal amount of information and data collection.
- HM2-Procedural

  There is more human intervention involved than in the last step, but the organization is still dependent upon using Threat Hunting procedures that other entities have

created; they still have not yet crafted their own set of
procedures as of yet.

■ HM3-Innovative

At this stage, the organization has created a minimal
set of Threat Hunting procedures on its own and is even
employing a small number of Threat Intelligence Hunters
to track down any potential adversaries.

■ HM4-Leading

The organization has now reached a point where they
have crafted their own complete set of Threat Hunting
procedures, and have even incorporated the use of automation into them.

Question 2

**One of the biggest threats that is now happening is that
of data leakage, whether it is intentional or not. How
would you specifically describe data leakage?**

In technical terms, especially as it relates to that of the
Threat Intelligence Hunter, data leakage can be defined as
the separation and/or the departure of a Data Packet from the
place where it was intended to be stored.

Question 3

**For the Threat Intelligence Hunter, knowing the poten-
tial sources of data leakage is a very crucial first step in
formulating an observable hypothesis. Can you tell me,
what are the top sources of data leakage?**

Yes, and they can be broadly categorized as follows:

■ Employee error (again, this could be nonintentional, but
this could stem from an Inside Attack as well)
■ Any unforeseen technological glitches from within the IT
Infrastructure
■ Server, workstation, or wireless device misconfigurations

- A Web-based application that was developed internally in an organization, but it was created using insecure Source Code
- Inadequate security controls that have been put into place at the organization

Question 4

What factors (or rather, pieces of information/data) would you consider when formulating a hypothesis that a data leakage incident is occurring?

I would look specifically at the following:

- Any risk profiles that have been created
- Any sort of impact and severity chart that relates to critical systems
- Any incident workflow diagrams that have been previously created (especially in the wake of previous Cyberattacks that may hit the business or the corporation)

Question 5

As a Threat Intelligence Hunter, you could also be very well working with Threat Intelligence Analysts. Can you describe in more detail the three types of Threat Intelligence Analysts?

In this kind of question, the recruiter wants to ascertain that you are fully aware of other job titles that are involved heavily in Threat Hunting as well. The three types of Intelligence Roles are as follows:

- Tactical Intelligence

    These individuals are heavily involved with examining the Network Infrastructure of an organization. They primarily work at Security Operations Centers (also known as SOCs) and spend time confirming any sorts of unusual behavior and adversaries that are trying to break through the lines of defense.

■ Operational Intelligence

These individuals spend much of their time trying to examine in close detail the operating environment of the corporation or business, focusing upon and sorting both internal and external threats.

■ Strategic Intelligence

These kinds of individuals are heavily involved with reporting findings to the C-Suite, in an easy-to-understand and comprehensible format, with a primary focus upon providing advice on Risk Management-based decisions, and the possible Return On Investment (ROI) on investing in newer types of Security Technologies.

Question 6

Suppose you have been asked by your CIO/CISO on what kind of Threat Hunting tools your team plans to use. He or she is not interested in tools that are developed in-house (primarily because they are fearful of the potential use of insecure Source Code); rather, they want a list of commercial products that are available. What would you recommend that they should invest in?

Very often, especially in Cybersecurity, people tend to become creatures of habit and like to stick to using the same tools repeatedly. The recruiter is trying to see if you can break away from this kind of habit, by testing your knowledge of the Threat Hunting tools that are out there, and that can be easily deployed in your organization. As of now, the top five Threat Hunting tools are as follows:

■ Sqrrl
■ Vectra Cognito
■ Infocyte Hunt
■ Exabeam Threat Intelligence Hunter
■ Endgame
■ DNIF

Question 7

Can you briefly describe the four most widely used Threat Hunting techniques?

Yes, they are as follows:

- Searching

   This can be regarded as probably the most basic form of Threat Hunting. With this technique, you are trying to support your formulated hypothesis with information and data from a very specific set of defined search criteria.
- Clustering

   This is more of a quantitative, statistical-based approach to Threat Hunting. With this technique, the Threat Intelligence Hunter is attempting to "cluster" similar datasets from a much larger, aggregate pool of data. In these situations, Machine Learning (ML) and Artificial Intelligence (AI) are tools that are used to accomplish this task, in an effort to find the hidden or unseen trends in these datasets.
- Grouping

   In this scenario, the Threat Intelligence Hunter is looking at different (or unique) artifacts that have been discovered and identifying them based on the same set of criteria that was used to formulate the original hypothesis.
- Stack Counting

   This is another type of statistical technique, in which the Threat Intelligence Hunter ascertains the total number of occurrences of a certain dataset by closely examining any sorts of outliers that may exist.

Question 8

Apart from the ATT&CK Threat Model that I have asked you about, what are some other Threat Hunting Models that can be used?

In this question, the recruiter is trying to gauge your understanding of other models that can be used to meet the Threat

Hunting needs of your organization. While the ATT&CK Framework is a very popular one that is used, there are others as well, such as the following:

- Lockheed Martin's Cyber Kill Chain
- FireEye's Attack Lifecycle
- Gartner's Cyber Attack Model

Question 9

How do you define Endpoint Detection and Response (EDR)?

While you have answered in a previous question that it is important to analyze multiple environments in an entire IT Infrastructure, the Threat Intelligence Hunter will also be called upon just to examine certain parts of it, especially the Endpoints. A definition of EDR is as follows:

> Endpoint detection and response (EDR) provides visibility into activity occurring on the network and endpoints by continuously monitoring activity for behavioral patterns that appear to be suspicious or anomalous. Data captured provides rich contextual information related to a threat to enable more efficient, prioritized remediation.
>
> **(Source: 5)**

In other words, you and your team are trying to find and determine if any potential Security risks exist where one point starts and where the other point ends within your entire IT Infrastructure.

Question 10

What are three important characteristics of an effective Threat Hunting tool?

You described the top 5 Threat Hunting Tools in a previous question, but this is a follow-up question to see what makes them so top of the breed. These products should contain, at minimum, the following characteristics:

- It must contain logs, such as Windows events logs, EDR logs, Anti-Virus logs, and Firewall/Proxy logs.
- It must have a SIEM, which stands for a "Security Information and Event Management" system. It must be centrally located in the tool for easy access and must be able to correlate all sorts of information and data in real time.
- A robust Analytics Engine, such as one that is Machine Learning (ML)- or Artificial Intelligence (AI)-based. It should be very effective in helping you and your Threat Hunting team find that "needle in the haystack".

The Characteristics of a Good Threat Hunter

1) *They should be able to handle an analytical-based interview*

Unlike other Cyber positions, you will be asking your candidate questions like what kind of analytical courses did they take in college, if they attended? This is important, as it shows they have the mindset of a potential scientist. If they answer with such things as calculus, encryption, cryptography, you know then you are golden. But keep in mind that simply taking analytical courses is not just the make or break for possible candidates. You also need to be asking them about the direct experiences that they have had with Threat Hunting, and how they approached it to find answers to questions. Heck, your candidate may not even have gone to college. But that should not disbar them. When interviewing candidates for a Threat Hunting position, try to bring in a member of the IT Security team as well who can ask more of the technical kinds of questions to probe their analytical thinking, and above all, to see if they could fit in well in the current environment. In this regard, you want your future Threat Hunter to think like an actual Cyberattacker, much like a Pen Tester would.

2) *They must be curious*

   Apart from being analytical, your candidate should also exhibit a strong sense of curiosity. Meaning along with knowing the difference between integrals and differentials (LOL), they must be curious about the world that is around them. Some great question to ask here is what kind of stuff do they like to read? How do they keep abreast of what is happening in the Cyber world? What motivates them? If you really want to test this, during the interview (perhaps in the second phase), you should pose to them a certain kind of Cyber scenario and ask them how they would find the answer to it, and what specific resources that they would use, apart from using Google. A good question to also ask here is what some of their favorite Cyber sites are. For me, being a tech writer, my favorite ones are those that bring reputable news stories and headlines. A key feature to look out for here is how the candidate looks at you when they respond to your curiosity-based questions. If they look you square in the eye, then you can tell for the most part that they are being honest. But if they tend to get squirmy, then that should be somewhat of a red flag to you.

Ok, now let's fast forward quite a bit and assume that you have found your ideal Threat Hunter. The next question that often arises, is how do you keep this talent to the best that you can? Well, here are some answers that could help:

1) *Create a social kind of atmosphere*

   By this, I don't mean to have a party every day at your office (but that may not be a bad thing either), but

encourage your Threat Hunters to work with others on
the IT Security team, and vice versa. Try to get your team
to share ideas among one another, and above all, share
that information and data as well. Let the Threat Hunters
know that you will be around for them, and they should
not feel afraid to speak their mind and ask for advice/
help when needed. From my experiences, Threat Hunters,
as mentioned previously, tend to be a rather shy bunch.
Try to break that mold away from them. Oh yea, and may
not hurt to take your team out to lunch or dinner every
few weeks to build these social skills.

2) *Let them do more*

By this I mean, don't limit the Threat Hunters to just
their specific job titles. Let them explore other avenues
as well. In other words, don't limit them. By nature,
Threat Hunters are explorers as well, and you should let
them explore your kingdom, within reason of course. Let
them go beyond their limits, and in the end, you will be
rewarded. In fact, this reminds me of the days when I
was a white belt in Taekwondo. One day, my instructor
said that all students could attempt to break a concrete
brick if they wanted to. I asked, does that also include
us, newbies? His reply was: "I do not limit students by
any means". So with those words, I broke the brick the
first time around, and boy, did that motivate me to even
higher levels.

3) *Always invest in and motivate your Threat Hunters*

We all know that the world of Cybersecurity is changing quickly and that your employees must be able to
keep up with this. Part of your job, in the end, is to give
them the tools to get that extra education. Yes, it can be
expensive. But this is something that you are going to
have to convince your CISO about. There may not be a
direct percentage ROI immediately when you provide this
training, but the chances are that happier employees will
be around with you the longest. And that can save time

and money right there because a high employee turnover not only is expensive but can also tarnish your company's image in the end. And always, whenever it is warranted, keep offering praise to your Threat Hunters. They are not used to it by nature, so a simple pat on the back or even a random $15 gift card to Starbucks or Panera Bread can go a long way to keep employees as well.

The Value of a Good Threat Hunter

But there is one job title which very often goes unnoticed, and when you first mention it, it leaves many people scratching their heads.

What is this Cyber job? Well, it is known as the "Threat Researcher". The roles of this job function are more or less what the title implies. These are the people that look at and review all of the threat intelligence that they receive on a daily basis. But to be clearer, Threat Intelligence can be defined as follows:

> Threat Intelligence is considered a new domain in cybersecurity that focuses on gathering intelligence and provides information to organizations related to APT (advanced persistent threats), different threat actors, tactics, and techniques used by special groups to attack that specific organization.

(Source: 6)

However, it is important to note that not just anybody can become a Threat Researcher. It takes a blend of both technical, analytical, and communications skills. But above all, it takes patience. A person must be able to sift through all of the evidence that they are presented with, dissect it, and from there make any hypotheses if a new threat variant is on the way, or there is actually one that is already about.

It can take time to do all of this, after all, the Threat Researcher does not want to sound the alarm bells off without substantial proof and evidence. Then, they must be able to crystallize their findings and report them in a way that not only the IT Security team can understand but even the higher-ups, such as those in the C-Suite and the Board of Directors.

Also, keep in mind that this is a hard job that can be very difficult to get unplugged from, just due to the sheer fact that there is so much information and data that is coming in on a daily basis. One can get burned out also.

But whatever the circumstances are, Threat Researchers are a vital component of the IT Security team, and their roles cannot be underestimated.

One of the better examples of this is the Threat Research team at Rapid 7. Their research at the time was heavily focused upon the improper configurations of the various Cloud platforms after a business moved their entire IT and Network Infrastructure into either the AWS or Microsoft Azure. It is important to keep in mind to never rely upon the default settings that are already set up when you first start the migration process.

They always need to be configured to what is unique to your needs and security environment. In this regard, the Threat Researchers from this company quickly detected and identified 121 Cloud-based misconfigurations. Of course, this could have led to huge amounts of confidential information and data being leaked, whether intentional or not.

In fact, it has even been cited that the average Threat Researcher discovers about ten potential security breaches a month, across well over fifteen industries. But luckily, these were remediated before they made the headlines.

It was also noted that about 25% of these potential breaches were caused by the right permissions not being established on the AWS server buckets (in technical terms, this is also known as the "S3").

In response to this, AWS has taken proactive steps to make all of these storage buckets private and encrypted when they are first deployed so that only authorized individuals can access them. But this does not apply to the older storage buckets that have been created in the AWS.

Because of this, IT Security teams have been advised by these Threat Researchers to double-check their configurations once again to make sure that they are compatible with their security policies.

This same team of Threat Researchers also discovered that the Healthcare Industry is also at grave risk, further substantiating the news headlines. Those datasets that are most at risk include those Personal Health Information (PHI) datasets, in which the predicted average for leakage could be as high as 10 million per potential security breach, with the high being estimated at 20 billion.

Even despite the tightening and enforcement of HIPAA, many healthcare organizations are still unable to really protect these PHI datasets to the best that they can. The primary reason cited for this by the Threat Researchers is the lack of the proper IT Security staff, and whatever is already in existence, these resources are already being taxed to their limits by fighting off both Ransomware and COVID-19 Cyber threat attack vectors.

Launching the Threat Hunting Exercise

Now that you have a team in place (at least theoretically), the next phase for your new Cybersecurity Consultancy is to launch your first Threat Hunting exercise. This section details what needs to be done.

The Risk Assessment – What Needs to Be Examined

In this first step, you are merely conducting intelligence activities as to which IT Assets are most at risk from the standpoint of a Cyberattack. This is often viewed by Cybersecurity professionals as the most important phase of any Threat Hunting activity. In this regard, there are nine key areas that need to be assessed:

1) *Threat and Vulnerability Management*

    In this segment, you are implementing a classification scheme in order to determine what is most at risk in your existing IT Infrastructure. In the end, all assets need to be examined, but in this specific scenario, you are using a top-down approach, by classifying those items that are at extremely high risk all the way down to those assets that are least at risk.

2) *Identity Management*

    In this part of the analysis, you and your IT Security staff are determining those mechanisms that have been implemented (or planned on being implemented) to confirm the identity of the employees that are trying to gain access to shared network resources. For example, do you make use of Password Managers, or Two-Factor Authentication (2FA)? Are more advanced technologies such as Biometrics (especially that of Fingerprint Recognition)?

3) *Security Awareness Training and Education*

    In this instance, you need to take a careful look as to how all of the employees in your business or corporation are being trained in protecting those IT resources that they use on a daily basis in order to conduct their job tasks. Also, this phase includes taking an audit as to what is being accessed the most, and if the proper rights and permissions have been established.

4) *The Security Policy*

    At this point, you and your IT Security staff need to carefully scrutinize the existing Security Policy that has been crafted and implemented. You need to address any weaknesses in this, and if it is even being enforced at all at your organization. You also need to confirm if this

Security Policy has been updated to reflect the current environment and needs of the organization, and if so, how often these updates took place.

5) *The Incident Response Plan:*

At this phase, the Incident Response Plan needs to be carefully audited as well. Some things that need to be examined are how often it has been updated, and if it has been practiced in real time. Also, you need to confirm if the employee contact information roster has also been updated, as well as how effective the Communications subcomponent of this Plan is.

6) *The Existing IT Infrastructure*

This is probably the most comprehensive as well as the most complex part of conducting this assessment. At this point, you and your IT Security Staff are trying to determine any vulnerabilities and weaknesses that currently exist in the current IT Infrastructure. You also need to conduct this same type of study on the existing Security Architecture that is in place.

7) *Security Management*

In this part, you are carefully scrutinizing your current IT Security staff. You are examining who is responsible for what in the overall Security Framework of your business or corporation, and how well and/or effective they have been in carrying out their duties when it comes to protecting and fortifying the current lines of defense(s).

8) *Emerging Security Technologies*

At this phase, you are taking a careful look as to what newer Security tools could be potentially implemented and/or upgraded in order to further beef up the lines of defenses at your organization. This also involves perhaps even conducting an analysis to determine if critical financial resources are being used in the most cost-effective manner. For example, rather than taking a "more spent is better" mindset is a much more "being selective in we deploy" attitude taking shape at your organization? This is a very crucial question to answer, because many business entities still have the viewpoint that simply spending money on deploying the latest Security Technologies in the greatest number possible will thwart off any sort of threat vector. This is a grave error in thinking, because you are simply increasing the attack surface for the Cyberattacker.

9) *The Use of Third-Party Vendors*

Making use of outsourced entities to conduct your daily business processes can carry a grave risk as well. In this instance, you need to carefully audit the selection process of hiring Third-Party Vendors, and if efforts are being currently being made to scrutinize their existing Security Processes to make sure that they come into alignment with the Security Requirements set forth by the CIO or CISO at your organization.

Once this Risk Assessment has been completed, the next step in any Threat Hunting Remediation exercise is determining what to exactly hunt for and the frequency of that hunt.

Determining What to Hunt For and How Often

After you and your IT Security staff have completed the Risk Assessment, the next step is to ascertain and finalize what kinds of threats or risks you need to specifically hunt for. There are four models that one utilizes, and they are as follows:

1) Lockheed Martin's Cyber Kill Chain
2) FireEye's Attack Lifecycle
3) Gartner's Cyber Attack Model
4) MITRE'S ATT&CK Lifecycle

It should be noted that it is the first model, the Cyber Kill Chain, which is the more popular one to use in any sort of Threat Hunting Remediation exercise. As its title implies, it was created and developed by Lockheed Martin back in 2011. The essential crux of this model is that when a Cyberattacker launches their particular threat, it usually happens in a series of phases, and at each of them, the threat vector could be potentially mitigated, provided that the right kinds of Security controls are in place.

These are the seven steps of the Kill Chain Model

1) *Reconnaissance*

   The Cyberattacker spends time to research their potential target or victim, determines their weaknesses and vulnerabilities, and determines the best way in (in other words, trying to find the most covert backdoor possible).

2) *Weaponization*

   The Cyberattacker creates their Malware Weapon to be deployed at the target or victim, which is designed specifically to match their vulnerabilities and/or weaknesses.

3) *Delivery*

   The Malware Weapon is now launched towards the target or victim.

4) *Exploitation*

   The malicious file in the Malware Weapon is now triggered, in order to take full advantage of the target's vulnerabilities and/or weaknesses.

5) *Installation*

   The Malware Weapon creates an access point or backdoor into the target, in order for the Cyberattacker to enter and further penetrate into.

6) *Command and Control*

   At this stage, the Cyberattacker literally now has his or her hands onto the target or victim and now can manipulate in any way they want to.

7) *Actions on Objective*

   Finally, the Cyberattacker takes the required actions in order to reach their desired objectives. For example, this could be the theft of passwords, ransomware, data exfiltration, data leakage, or even the destruction of data.

After you have selected the appropriate model you wish to utilize, you must then decide which of the risks are deemed to be at the highest level or the most concerning to your organization. This has already been determined when you completed the Risk Assessment.

Next, you have to ascertain the kinds of activities that a Cyberattacker could use to launch their threat vectors at these particular risks and map them accordingly to the various phases of the model you have chosen to use.

For example, if it has been determined that the Network Servers in your IT Infrastructure are most at risk (based upon the results of the Risk Assessment), you and your IT Security staff would then determine the kinds of actions or activities that a Cyberattacker would take to launch an attack against them. You would then place them at the different phases of the Kill Chain Model (assuming you have decided to use this model).

Finally, you then need to determine and set up a timetable (or calendar) as to how often you plan to conduct your Threat Hunting Remediation exercises. It is recommended that you conduct these as often as possible, by rotating through the different IT Assets that are most at risk.

The exact frequency will be ultimately determined by the availability of the resources that you have at hand, but it is very important not to keep repeating the same Threat Hunting Remediation exercise repeatedly.

Launching the Threat Hunting Remediation Exercise

After you have determined the activities that a Cyberattacker would use to launch their threat vectors against your most risk IT Assets, the next step is to actually conduct the Threat Hunting Remediation exercise. There are four general components that are associated with this, and they are as follows:

1) *Creating and testing a hypothesis*

In this step, you and your IT Security staff are trying to determine the results that you are expecting from conducting a Hunting exercise.

Once again in our example with regards to the Network Servers in the last section, a potential hypothesis is that if a fileless-based attack is launched it would then totally wipe out the memory banks of the Network Servers, thus totally eradicating their processing capabilities of them.

2) *Collecting the relevant information and data*

Next, you will want to follow up with your hypothesis by investigating it with the Threat Hunting tools that you have available to you, and collecting the information/data that is yielded from it. For example, some things to be on the lookout for include any anomalies, and malicious patterns in the datasets that have been compiled. These then could be potentially used to reconstruct the Cyberattacker's Tactics, Techniques, and Procedures (aka TTPs). Also, if no anomalies are detected, you could then potentially rule out that no systems have been compromised.

3) *Determining the steps that can be completed by Automation*

Once you have completed the last step, you then need to determine which steps can be carried out by Automated Threat Hunting tools. As it was mentioned earlier, you don't want to waste your IT Security staff's valuable time by conducting the same Threat Hunting Remediation exercise over and over again manually. A good rule of thumb here is that if the same Hunting exercise needs to be repeated again at a subsequent point in time, then it should be completely automated as much as possible; manual processes should be used only for brand-new Hunting exercises.

4) *Plan a course of action*

After you have compiled the relevant information and data in the second step, the next step is to determine what happens next. If the analyses of the patterns and anomalies indicate that a Cyberattack is in its beginning stages, then this needs to be handed over to the Incident Response Team so that the threat can be mitigated as quickly as possible. Or, if no threat is detected, then you need to determine what the next Threat Hunting Remediation exercise will be.

Determining the Effectiveness of the Threat Hunting Exercise

After each and every Threat Hunting Remediation exercise, you and your IT Security staff must gauge the effectiveness of it, and determine if it was successful or not. Thus, it is important to establish a set of Key Performance Indicators, or KPIs, as a benchmark to go off of. The following are some KPIs that you can use to assess the effectiveness of your Hunting exercises:

1) *Number of Incidents by Severity*

With this, you are keeping a running tally of the total number of both known and unknown incidents that are occurring in your organization. After a period of time, this will give you some context as to how well the lines of defense are working in your organization.

2) *Number of hosts that have been compromised*

Just like above, you are also keeping a running tally as to the total number of compromised Hosts that still exist in the IT Infrastructure. This is a useful metric especially when you run Hunting exercises on your Endpoint

Security tools, as it can reveal any potential setting misconfigurations.

3) *The Dwell Time*

This metric reflects how long discovered Cyber threats have been active in your IT Infrastructure. Within this, there are three areas that need to be specifically addressed:

a. The time from infection until detection;

b. The time from detection until to investigation;

c. The time from investigation to remediation.

4) *The number of vulnerabilities identified*

Like the first two KPIs, with this one, you are keeping track of the total number of vulnerabilities you are discovering, based upon the Hunting exercises that you are conducting.

5) *The number of insecure practices corrected and identified*

This particular metric gives you an idea of the total number of IT-related Insecure Practices that are occurring at your organization. Obviously, by identifying them, you should be able to correct them quickly so that they do not become a potential backdoor for any future Cyberattacks.

6) *The False Positive Rate of Transitioned Hunts*

As mentioned earlier in this article, once you have completed a particular Threat Hunting Remediation exercise, and if you have to repeat it again at a subsequent point in time, you will want to automate as much the processes that were involved with it. Once this automation process has been used, this particular metric will then give the total number of False Positives that have been generated. This will give you an idea of where future improvements need to be made.

Finally, it is important to keep in mind that the overall Threat Hunting Remediation processes as detailed here are general in nature – they will obviously have to be tailored to the unique Security Requirements of your business or corporation.

Further Reading

1. https://www.raytheon.com/sites/default/files/cyber/rtnwcm/ groups/iis/documents/content/proactive-hunting-datasheet.pdf
2. https://www.darkreading.com/partner-perspectives/juniper/ proactive-threat-hunting-taking-the-fight-to-the-enemy-/a/d-id /1331084
3. https://go.crowdstrike.com/rs/281-OBQ-266/images/Whitepa perProactiveHunting.pdf
4. https://digitalguardian.com/blog/what-threat-hunting-emerging -focus-threat-detection
5. https://www.bloorresearch.com/technology/endpoint-detection -and-response/
6. https://cybertalents.com/blog/what-is-required-to-work-in-threat -intelligence-jobs

Chapter 4

Staying Ahead of the Competition

As you launch and continue to grow your Cybersecurity Consultancy, it is always important for you to stay ahead of your peers. One way to do this is to obtain those certifications (also known as "Certs") that will give you that advantage. There are tons of them available today in the Cybersecurity Industry, so you need to focus on those that will bring the most value to your Cybersecurity Consultancy and also you. Everybody has their views on them, as do I, but this is one of the first things that a prospect will look at. The bottom line here is, don't get caught up with how many certs you have, but focus on those that bring quality and relevance to you.

The Top Five Certs

1) *The CISSP*

This is an acronym that stands for the "Certified Information Security Systems Professional". In fact, it is one of the oldest certs out there, but it is still

DOI: 10.1201/9781003305309-4

one of the most highly regarded and well-respected ones available. If you take a look at some of the Cybersecurity job boards, you will notice that many of the specialty types of positions require that you have the CISSP. This cert is offered through the ISC2. In order to be able to take the exam for this cert, you must have the following requirements:

a. At least five years of professional work experience in Cybersecurity. This experience must be in at least two of the eight knowledge domains that the exam covers. However, if you have a degree (even an advanced one), this will count as only one year against the work requirement.

b. If you do not meet all the work experience requirements, you can still take the exam. However, you just won't receive the actual CISSP immediately after passing. Instead, you will become what is known as an "Associate of the ISC2", and from there, you will have up to six years to gain the relevant experience. The knowledge domains that the CISSP exam covers can be seen in the following matrix:

Domain	Body of Knowledge
Domain 1	Security and Risk Management
Domain 2	Asset Security
Domain 3	Security Architecture and Engineering
Domain 4	Communication and Network Security
Domain 5	Identity and Access Management (IAM)
Domain 6	Security Assessment and Testing
Domain 7	Security Operations
Domain 8	Software Development Security

Here are some other exam details that you should be aware of:

a. The length of the exam is three hours;
b. It consists primarily of multiple-choice questions;
c. A passing is deemed to be 700 points out of a possible total of 1,000 points;
d. The exam can be taken at just about any ISC2-authorized or Pearson VUE-testing center;
e. The cost of the exam is $699.00.

After you have passed the exam, you have to sign a document claiming that you will adhere to the ISC Code of ethics. You will also have to have a CISSP professional vouch for and confirm your work experience. Once you have received the actual cert, there is a $125.00 annual maintenance fee, and you must earn at least 40 Continuing Professional Education (CPEs) credits on an annual basis as well, for a three-year cycle.

2) *The CompTIA Security+*

This particular cert has also been around for quite some time. In fact, it is deemed to be the first security-related one that most Cybersecurity professionals should obtain before embarking upon other specialist certs. It is also compliant with the standards set forth by the ISO 10724 and is even approved to meet the stringent requirements of the 8140/8570.01-M as established by the Department of Defense (DoD).

Unlike the CISSP, there is no minimum work experience required to take the exam. But it is highly recommended that you have two years of work experience in IT Security (it does not necessarily have to be Cybersecurity, per se). Here are some of the skills that you will be tested on for this cert:

a. The ability to conduct a general type of security assessment and recommend the appropriate solutions;
b. Your knowledge about Cloud-based platforms; the Internet of Things (IoT); and Mobile Security;

c. Awareness of the Federal Regulations (such as the GDPR, CCPA, HIPAA, etc.);
d. Your ability to respond to and analyze certain types of security-related incidents.

The following matrix provides more of the exam particulars:

Total number of questions	90
Type of question asked	Multiple-choice
Passing score	Minimum of 750 (based upon a scale of 100–900)
Testing venue	Any Pearson VUE-Testing Centers
Cost of exam	$399.00
Renewal requirements	Earning of at least 50 CPEs in a three-year cycle

3) *The CompTIA CySA+*

There are a lot of job openings out there which have the title "Cybersecurity Analyst". This is a very broad title, and there are a lot of candidates who apply for these kinds of positions. In order to separate yourself from the rest of the crowd, you need a cert that will give you that unique advantage. One who will do the trick is known as the "Cybersecurity Analyst+", and it is a relatively new one that is currently being offered by CompTIA.

Its primary focus is to test your ability on how well you can capture network traffic data and analyze it in real time. It has an emphasis on the usage of automation and threat hunting tools, and the compliance frameworks of the GDPR, CCPA, HIPAA, etc. There are also other skills that will be tested, and these include:

a. The ability to properly position the various intelligence resources available today;
b. Your knowledge of how to identify and react to certain types of threat vectors;

c. How well you can advise the IT Security team to recover from various kinds of security breaches (this includes Incident Response, Disaster Recovery, and Business Continuity).

The following chart illustrates more specifics about the exam you need to take in order to obtain this kind of cert:

Exam code	CS0-002
Number of questions	85 total questions
Question type	Multiple-choice and "performance-based"
Time limit for the test	165 minutes
Passing score needed	Minimum of 750 (based on a scale of 100–900)
Testing centers	Pearson VUE
Cost of exam	$395.00

It should be noted that there is no mandatory work experience level required, but it is highly suggested that you have at least 3–4 years of relevant experience. The CySA+ has been designed to follow the Security+ cert, so it is also advised that you have obtained this first.

This cert also has a three-year cycle like Security+, and in order to keep it, you have to have a minimum of at least 60 CPEs during this timeframe.

4) *The CCSP*

This acronym stands for the "Certified Cloud Security Professional", and it too is also offered by ISC2. This kind of cert is deemed to be much more technically oriented when compared to the CISSP. It has been specifically designed for those individuals who want to further their careers in the area of Cloud Security. To take the exam for this cert, you must possess a minimum of at least five years of work experience, which is broken down as follows:

a. Three years in the realm of Information Security;

b. One year in one of the six knowledge domains.

The matrix below illustrates these specific domains:

Domain	Body of Knowledge
Domain 1	Cloud Concepts, Architecture, and Design
Domain 2	Cloud Data Security
Domain 3	Cloud Platform and Infrastructure Security
Domain 4	Cloud Application Security
Domain 5	Cloud Security Operations
Domain 6	Legal, Risk, and Compliance

Just like the CISSP, if you do not have enough work experience, you can become an Associate of the ISC2 until you gain it. After you have passed the exam, your work experience must be vouched for by another professional who also has the CCSP cert, and you must also prescribe to and adhere to the ISC2 Code of Ethics.

The table below provides more details about the exam:

Type of exam	Multiple-choice
Duration of the exam	Four hours
Exam questions	Total of 125
Exam cost	$599.00
Testing centers	Any Pearson VUE center; remote testing is also available from your own home

In order to maintain your cert, you must earn a minimum of 90 CPEs throughout a three-year cycle and pay a $125 Annual Maintenance Fee (AMF).

5) *The CISM*

This acronym stands for the "Certified Information Security Manager". As its name implies, this cert is specifically for those individuals that want to eventually further their managerial position in the world of Cybersecurity. It is offered through an organization known as the "Information Systems Audit and Control Association", or "ISACA" for short. In order to take this exam, you must possess at least five years of work-related experience. You must have this experience from within the last ten years from when you first applied to take the exam.

There are circumstances in which waivers can be offered for a two-year period. There are four knowledge domains that are covered by the CISM, which are as follows:

a. Information Security Governance;
b. Information Risk Management;
c. Information Security Program Development and Management;
d. Information Security Incident Management.

The table below provides more details about the exam:

Type of exam	Multiple-choice
Number of questions	150 total
Duration of exam	4 hours total
Passing score needed	450 points out of a total of 800 points
Cost of exam	$575.00 for ISACA members; $760.00 for nonmembers
Testing centers	Any PSI-testing venue

Just like the other certs reviewed, the CISA credential is good for a three-year time period. In order to maintain this, you must earn at least 20 CPEs on an annual basis during this time span. Also, there is an annual maintenance fee of $45.00 for ISACA members and $85.00 for nonmembers. Also, you must prescribe and adhere to the ISACA's Code of Professional Ethics.

The Different Ways to Prepare for a Cybersecurity Certification

1. *Going to a boot camp*

   When one hears this term, the image of revelry sounding to start off the day often comes to mind. But relax, you will not have to go through rigorous calisthenics or listen to a drill sergeant. Instead, you will have to survive daylong and very intensive classes that can be mentally grueling, to say the least. Most Cybersecurity cert boot camps are about a weeklong (typically five business days), and the goal of them is to teach you all that you need to know in order to pass the exam for your desired certification shortly after it is over. Typically, these kinds of boot camps are a blend of both classroom instruction and hands-on practical training in order to get you as prepared as possible for the exam. While the pass rate can be deemed to be high, boot camps are also very expensive. They can range anywhere from $2,000.00 to $20,000.00 total (depending upon how long the boot camp is – some are even offered over the course of 2–3 months). Worst yet, the fees are not refundable, so if you don't pass the exam on the first attempt, you may need to do it all over again. Boot camps can be not only very advantageous but also very costly in the end, with no guarantees.

2. *Online Instruction*

   If you cannot afford the cost of a boot camp, there is yet another option that is available to you. Many vendors of the more popular certifications offer online training for just a fraction of the cost (typically, most of them run only for about a few hundred dollars). With this approach, you get access to live instruction from an experienced professional. Plus, the instructional lessons are broken up into several modules. You also get practice quizzes and exams, and even hands-on lab experience as well in many instances. The other advantage of this approach is that you can more or less learn at your own pace, especially if you have a hectic schedule both personally and professionally.

3. *Self-study*

If any of the approaches just reviewed do not fit your bill, there is one more option: Studying on your own. With this, you are embarking on teaching everything to yourself that you need to know in order to prepare for the exam. The most popular way to do this is to purchase a book and start reading/taking notes. But keep in mind, purchasing these kinds of materials through the certification vendor can also be expensive. Rather, your best bet is to find comparable books from Amazon or even look for books at your local library. With this method, time is literally at your side. You can take as much time as you want to learn the material, and you can sign up for the exam when you feel that you are ready for it. But the downside here is that you have to be motivated and highly disciplined on a regular basis in order to help ensure that you will pass the exam on the first attempt. To help you do this, it is always best to form a study group with others who are also taking the same exam. Also keep in mind that there are also plenty of free flash cards, quizzes, and other study aids that you can download for free to aid in your preparation.

Be On Top of the Hiring Curve

Even today, there is a drastic shortage of Cybersecurity workforce. The problem is there are no motivated and eager candidates to fill these roles, but companies are extremely picky in who they want to hire. In other words, they only want the cookie-cutter candidate who will fit the exact requirements. But unfortunately, this is not going to happen. So, one way that you can keep your brand-new Cybersecurity Consultancy ahead of your competition is by hiring those workers; while they may not have a lot of Cybersecurity experience, they are definitely motivated and willing to learn, which I think are among some of the most traits and characteristics in hiring a good Cybersecurity worker. Here is how it is done.

Introduction

A huge Cyber problem that is compounding Corporate America is the lack of a solid Cybersecurity workforce. While there are skilled workers out there, it is simply not enough today. IT Security teams are now being stretched well beyond their breaking points, and the burnout rate has probably reached its highest level than ever before.

Consider some of these key findings to further illustrate this severity:

- Worldwide, there is a total of over 4.07 million Cybersecurity jobs to be filled.
- There are 561,000 jobs that remain unfilled here in the United States.
- There are also 2.6 million jobs that also remain unfilled in the APAC region.
- The European Union (EU) has reported a complete, 100% deficit in their Cybersecurity workforce.
- 65% of businesses worldwide have reported that they lack solid Cybersecurity workers.
- There has to be at least 145% growth rate in terms of hiring to fill this shortage at least minimally.
- 51% of companies have reported that they are at risk of a major Cyberattack because of the lack of Cybersecurity workers.

(Source: 1)

What Is the Solution???

1) *Hire the young college graduates*

At least here in Corporate America, the trend is to hire only seasoned Cybersecurity professionals. The primary reason for this is that companies want only individuals with deep levels of experience to protect their digital assets. To a certain degree, this is understandable. But keep in mind, this is a double-edged sword. For example, if only seasoned professionals are entrusted to safeguard the crown jewels of a business, you will still experience a lack of good workers. The reason for this is that if you only want the "best of the best", you are going to have to offer a very lucrative compensation and benefits package. This, of course, can take a hit on the bottom line, especially during rough times like the COVID-19. Because of this, your seasoned and most entrusted workers will burn out very quickly, quit, look for another job, or even start their own business. In the end, there is nothing to be gained. So, you have to take that chance and hire much younger workers who will most likely be fresh out of college or some kind of cert program. In this regard, it is important to think about the long-term effects. If you do hire a college graduate and train them to protect your mission-critical information and data, the chances are greater that they will feel a stronger sense of loyalty and, perhaps, even be your employee for a very long time.

2) *Hire outsourced talent*

With the gig economy now in almost full swing, there are many Cybersecurity workers who are available on a contract basis. A typical example of this is the "vCISO". This is where you hire experienced, third-party individuals to literally be your CISO for a fixed-term contract. The primary benefit of this is that you do not have to pay an exorbitant salary or benefits package; you just pay a flat fee, which is typically around a few thousand dollars. These individuals will offer candid, neutral, and unbiased advice as to how your company needs to better fortify its lines of defense. More than likely, they will also have other contacts that help to further augment your existing IT Security staff, especially in the way of conducting Penetration Testing and Threat Hunting exercises and providing security training for your other, non-IT employees. Although it would be nice to have a permanent, full-time staff that you can always count on, hiring contractors is also a great way to go, especially if you do not have the budget to do this. For example, with outsourced employees, you can quickly ramp up or ramp down your staffing needs, especially if you are an SMB. But there is one especially important thing to keep in mind: If you are looking at hiring contractors, you have to make sure that they are as fully vetted as possible. There are two reasons for this: (1) You are entrusting them to the databases of where the Personal Identifiable Information (PII) of your customers is stored; and (2) If one of these contractors makes a mistake which leads up to a security breach, they will not be liable for it, you will be.

3) *Make use of automated tools*

One of the other factors that is stretching IT Security teams to their limits is that on a daily basis, they are being bombarded with tons of alerts and warning messages from all of the security tools/technologies they have deployed. At the present time, most businesses in Corporate America have to triage all of these items on a manual basis, which can take hours, if not days. Because of this, those alerts/warnings that are legitimate very often fall through the cracks, thus exposing the business to an even greater risk of becoming a victim of a large-scale Cyberattack. In this regard, you should seriously consider making use of Artificial Intelligence (AI), especially in the way of Neural Networks. With this, you can quickly and seamlessly automate this process, because they can filter for and discard the false positives, and only present those alerts/ warnings that appear to be legitimate. Keep in mind that AI-based solutions are actually very affordable these days; many of them come as hosted offerings via the Cloud. In turn, this makes deploying them pretty easy. But best of all, they are also scalable, to fit your needs. The bottom line is that your existing IT Security employees will not be so overburdened and, thus, will be on their A-game when it comes to protecting your business.

4) *Consider hiring those Cyberattackers who have turned over to the "Good Side"*

Yes, it is quite possible like in the Return Of The Jedi with Darth Vader, that Cyberattackers can turn over a leaf and become what is known as "Ethical Hackers". In this instance, they are often hired for bug bounty programs that are offered by some of the largest IT companies, including the likes of Oracle, Microsoft, Apple, Google, etc. They are called upon to break the new applications that these companies offer to discover any unknown vul- nerabilities, gaps, weaknesses, backdoors, etc. In return, if something is found and a solution is offered to fix it, they are paid a huge bonus, very often ranging payouts in the five or even six figures. As a result, you should look into hiring these kinds of individuals. After all, you want employees who think exactly like a Cyberattacker, so why not hire people who have actually done it? To do this, you can reach out to these bigger companies and advertise any open Cyber-related positions that you may have. Or, if you have some extra money on hand, you could also perhaps even deploy your own bug bounty program, and if you are impressed enough with the Ethical Hacker, then you should probably hire them on board.

5) *Start to create internships and/or apprenticeship programs*

Remember, it is especially important to spark a deep level in Cybersecurity when individuals are at an incredibly young age, especially when they are in their teens, especially if they are in junior high or high school. For example, you can partner up with your local college, university, and/or even high school and offer various sorts of internships, summer camps, etc. to prospective students. If some of them turn out to exceed your expectations, perhaps you can even be a mentor to them as they enter college, and continue working with them so that you can even hire them as employees for your company after they graduate. One key thing you should also consider is to offer some sort of financial help in the way of training or taking the actual exam if they are interested in obtaining a Cybersecurity certification that is relevant to your company.

Further Reading

1. https://www.infosecurity-magazine.com/news/cybersecurity-skills-shortage-tops/

Index

Printed in the United States
by Baker & Taylor Publisher Services